PLEASANT COMPANY ACCEPTED

PLEASANT COMPANY
ACCEPTED

❋ ❋ ❋ ❋ ❋

Rita Anton

Drawings by Burmah Burris

DOUBLEDAY & COMPANY, INC.

GARDEN CITY, NEW YORK

1964

"Keeping the Records Straight" previously appeared in *America* whose editors have permitted its inclusion here.

To

my mother and father

with love

With deep appreciation to Gerald Ellard, S.J., Caroline Ward, Sister Mary St. Matthew, B.V.M., Mrs. Eleanor McEnery, Mrs. Virginia McCarthy, and John W. Christian, S.J., for the valuable advice and assistance so generously given.

Contents

8   CONTENTS

PLEASANT COMPANY ACCEPTED

Nana

Someone aptly described a man as the head of the home, and a woman as its heart. My mother was more than that; she was the hub and center of all our activities. Dad deferred to her in every matter. She cooked our meals, washed and sewed our clothes, cleaned the house, and in addition to rearing seven children, taught school.

Mother was packaged small, like that little atomic unit that activates the submarine *Nautilus*. She came from healthy Irish stock that tended to consider illness a disgrace. Her mother, my Grandma Kelly, lived with us during most of our childhood. Grandma's theory was, if you're not feeling well, try not to think about it; concentrate on your work and the illness will give up and leave. Above all, counseled Grandma, never go to bed and coddle a germ. This sets up a chain reaction within the family; someone will call the doctor, who will dose you with medicine, and then there is no recourse but to be sick, swallow the medicine, and convalesce slowly.

Mother inherited Grandma's superb good health, which was compounded of a healthy mental outlook on life, and a firm belief in the goodness of God. Grandma lived to see her ninety-fifth birthday. Mother, who is now grandmother to twenty-seven children, is planning a trip to Europe with Dad. She looks at least fifteen years younger than her actual age, and shows promise of outstripping Grandma's record for a peaceful and happy longevity.

Mother was the practical one in our family. She learned early to compartmentalize and organize her life in order to provide time for all the things she had to do. She had the household organized so that the cleaning was accomplished without fuss or flutter. She had regular times for shopping, mending, and ironing, and the will power to stick to them. Budgeting too, was her department, and by some miracle I have never been able to penetrate, she juggled the salary money so that it covered everything necessary for seven children, as well as good educations for all. Not a dime was spent for luxury items. No money was dribbled away on expensive entertaining or liquor. Neither of my parents used it, nor did they serve alcoholic drinks to their guests. Coffee, ice cream, and cake were the standard menu when visitors came.

When Dad took the children excursioning, Mother used this time to catch up on jobs that had been waiting. Sometimes we would come home to find her looking fresh and clear-eyed after a nap; but more often we would return to find that she had painted one of the bedrooms. For time was a precious commodity to my mother; she wasted none of it. I never saw her leaning over the back fence chatting with the neighbors. She was always pleasant, and brief with them. Mother believed that most neighborhood squabbles began because people got too familiar. The neighbors respected Mother. She smiled easily, kept a clean home, and never permitted her children to annoy anyone. We were neatly dressed, and clean. The neighbor's property was as sacred to us as if there had been a ring of fire around it. Whenever an argument between children got loud enough for Mother to hear it indoors, she would go to the front door and quietly call us all in for the remainder of the day. She seldom probed into the matter at all, and we learned not to bother her with it. The point was, loud arguments and fighting were vulgar, and we were not permitted to indulge in them. As a result, we grew up without enemies, and were lucky enough to have many good friends.

My father, too, had a great aversion to gossip. He used to go to great lengths to avoid the company of a woman who had a passion for pointing out the faults of all the other neighbors. She attended the same morning Mass that he did, and frequently Dad was forced to walk home with her, grimly trying to keep his temper while she related with great animation the latest foibles she had uncovered. One morning Dad stopped her cold. She was waiting for him on the church steps, and had just launched into "Have you heard the latest?" when my father tipped his hat to her and said in a dignified voice:

"I'm sorry I can't speak to you this morning; I still have the Host in my mouth."

Mother managed to sandwich in a great deal of instruction while she went about her daily work. She gave us our baths every evening to the accompaniment of the multiplication tables. Briskly rubbing our backs with the soapy cloth, she would be murmuring, "Six times six?", and if we answered correctly, she would go on to six times seven, and so on. Our homework was done en masse at the dining-room table every evening. Mother would be hovering nearby in the kitchen, keeping an ear cocked for questions and maintaining order. Sometimes she had to curb Dad, who was eager to teach us cube root at the age of seven. My father was wonderful at math, and none of us took after him. Perhaps he tried too hard to interest us when we were very young. But they both entered into the homework as if it were their own. Mother wanted to see the compositions before we turned them in; if there were erasures or misspelled words, we had to redo them. Neither of them ever gave us an answer. Those we had to figure out ourselves; but they opened every door they could to throw more light on the subject for us.

Mother encouraged us to use the books at home to discover what was termed "outside information." The sisters at school placed much value on this extra work, and we were given credit for it. She asked Dad to bring home slides from the library to round out our general knowledge as each new country loomed into our consciousness via the geography book. These slides showed us how the people looked, what the general physical features of the country were, and fascinating glimpses of the costumes and customs.

When we studied the Civil War in history, Dad brought home the movie *The Birth of A Nation.* This was to be a Halloween treat for us: educational, and cannily calculated to keep us off the street on an evening which might be perilous for young children. The trick-or-treat brigade began ringing the doorbell around eight o'clock, and when they were admitted for their candy and saw the movie, they didn't want to leave. Dad claims that every time he lit the lamp to change a reel there were ten more kids in the living room. All I know is, Mother passed around popcorn, and when that gave out, the trick-or-treat bags were raided, and we were all limp with the emotional impact of the Civil War story and a volatile mixture of food.

My mother had a profound respect for the teaching nuns. Whenever difficulties arose at school, which was seldom, she always assumed that Sister was right. "If you had been paying attention and doing your work," she would say wisely, "you wouldn't have gotten into trouble." Having been on the same side of the desk gave her a real sympathy for the sisters who had to deal with a roomful of lively children. I never heard either of my parents speak disrespectfully of any of our teachers.

We were, as a consequence, relieved of the responsibility of judging the comparative merits of the sisters, or giving pert little critiques of their ability which seem to occupy so much of a student's time today.

Someone has described the art of parenthood in this way: "First you teach them to crawl, and then to walk; and then you teach them to walk away from you." My mother cut the apron strings as soon as she saw we were capable of walking by ourselves. We were always conscious that her advice and support were there if we needed it, but we knew that she expected us to think for ourselves. She never extricated us from mistakes. We were left to free ourselves and learn from them.

As one after another of us married and left home, we left with her smile and blessing. There were no maudlin tears over "losing my baby." Mother made certain that we had left babyhood when we reached the age of reason. She welcomed our marriage partners with a joy and graciousness that has made her a favorite with every one of them. In twenty years of our marriage, my mother never once ventured an opinion on decisions made by my husband and me. When we wanted advice, we had but to ask, and we knew it would be sound, seasoned, and simple. But if we had decided to paint the house in polka dots, Mother would have remained silent on the matter.

After thirty-five years of teaching in the Chicago public schools, Mother decided to retire. Typically, retirement means that she spends most of her time sitting with her grandchildren. None of us has to worry about help when we go to the hospital for a new baby, or with a sick member of the family. Mother is there almost before she's asked, cheerfully, capably, and urging us out the door with "now don't worry about a thing; everything will be just fine here." During vacations, the youngest child is always left in Mother's care. She has a little nursery set up in her home to accommodate the very young grandchildren. She keeps a large box of toys in the front hall closet for the older group. The children all call her "Nana"; she is their favorite person on earth.

Mother is one of those rare people who gets her greatest happiness from giving joy to others. The first week we were married, and were getting settled in our apartment, Mother phoned me to say she was sending over a little gift for Al and me, "something I know that you'll both love." I was shortsighted at the time, and the only thing I could think of that would add to my bliss was an electric mixer. "Nope," said Mother, "but it should be delivered today, so be sure you wait at home for it." About an hour later two men came struggling up the apartment staircase with a beautiful little spinet piano—an addition to our home that we thought we would have to wait five years to acquire. We both loved it; our children learned to play it as each reached the proper age. Mother comes to listen to them. When I see her face lit with pleasure at the sound of their music, I know that her generosity has been repaid at least in part. But who can ever repay the generosity of a wonderful mother completely?

Mother took her job of parenthood seriously. She knew that she would have to answer to God for each of us, and she taught us tirelessly, patiently, and continually. But

many of the most powerful lessons I learned from her
were by example, rather than words. Grandma Kelly, her
mother, lived with us for about thirty years. The gentle
conversation that flowed between mother and daughter
remains in my memory still. I never heard a hasty or un-
kind word pass between them. They were both hard-
working women, both mothers of large families, and they
had a mutual respect for one another that showed in
everything they did and said.

Grandma Kelly had been born on a farm near Dubuque,
Iowa. When we were little, she used to tell us stories
about that far-off time. My brother Bill, the youngest,
sat in her lap by the hour listening to her stories. She
remembered seeing the fiery blaze in the sky over Chicago
when the Great Fire occurred. She was a little girl at the
time, and she said she was seated on the front porch of
the farmhouse when she noticed that the night sky over
Chicago was all red and queer. She called the others, and
they watched it for hours. The news of the disaster didn't
reach the Iowa farm until two weeks later. Grandma's
father had been instrumental in bringing the first priest
to that section of Iowa. The priest lived with them until
he got established. Just down the road from their farm was
the Monastery of New Mellary, where the Trappists lived,
Grandma tells of seeing them in the woods in the early
mornings, felling trees. She told us, too, of the First Communion gift her father bought for her. He had arranged
to have a piano sent up the Mississippi from St. Louis to
Dubuque, where it was carted overland on a wagon to her
home. She says it was the first piano to arrive in the
county. People came from miles around to see it. Grandma
learned to play the piano at the Convent of the Visitation
in Virginia, where she attended school. She still remem-

bered "Nellie Grant's Wedding March" and played it for us when she was eighty-five. It is possible that Grandma's memory of this great gift stayed with my mother, and made her duplicate it for me. It is a tradition I should love to carry on for my daughter.

Mother and Dad are leaving soon for the trip to Europe they have been waiting for all their lives. They have seen much of America since the last child left home; travel, so long denied them, has all the wonder of a new toy for them now. They go junketing blithely about the country, sampling food, loving the sights, meeting new people, and having a ball. Europe will thrill them, even if it rains all the while they're there. They will pray at all the shrines, stroll down Parisian streets, gad about Florence, inspect the Alps and the Rhine, and love every moment of it.

Mother and Dad remind me of the Beatitudes. The promises have come true. The humble, meek, and clean of heart have inherited the earth and the blessings of heaven.

The South Side

The deep South is an unknown to me. I have never rambled south of the Mason-Dixon; never indeed, as far south as Springfield, Illinois. But I have been to the South Side of Chicago, where I am told, there are not a few resemblances to Dixie. My paternal grandparents and Aunt Marguerite lived on the far South Side, and many Sunday afternoons found the seven little Kenters plus their intrepid male guide boarding the Addison Street bus for the Loop, where, after the necessary stops for regurgitation and drinks of water, we would climb the El stairs for the big push south. To this day I cannot recall the exact route. The whole fifteen years of trips south have jelled into a frightful miasma of nausea, cinders in the eye, and ringing in the ears.

My sister Virginia, a social type, always wanted to sit behind the bus driver, and glean from him, by astute questioning, his name, number of offspring, and whether or not he enjoyed his work. Twenty minutes or so was usually

sufficient to obtain a complete file on the helpless pilot. Then Virginia would amble back, find a partially open window in which to place her nose and ride out the remainder of the journey in happy contemplation.

I had no such master plan. I was the oldest, and chief trouble shooter for Dad, who had his hands full trying to watch the little boys. At least once each trip I would notice Loretta or Rosemary turning green and would alert Dad (at the back of the bus) so that the evacuation order might be given.

During these lengthy journeys across the city, my father was frequently subjected to keen embarrassment; the worst of these instances possibly being the time the poor man heard his paternity called into question. We had spread all over the vehicle, of necessity, since it was rare that we could find eight seats together. Loretta and George selected the rear of the El, Virginia was chatting companionably with the motorman, Tom and Rosemary sat near Dad in the middle of the train, and Billy and I had one of the long side seats. An El train is generally noisy, but George's voice, at five, had a clarion quality. He lifted it bravely over the din of travel, and yelled across the train to Dad.

"Hey, Dad—aren't you our real father?" My father, feigning deafness, looked fixedly out the window, but George the intrepid raised his voice four decibels higher.

"Hey, Dad—it's me, back here!" Dad twisted around, hoping to squelch further conversation with his famous look. Distance, however, had robbed it of its usual effectiveness.

"Aren't you our *real* father, Dad?" My father nodded a vigorous affirmative, while the other passengers listened with spellbound attention. George considered for a moment.

"Well, Loretta says you're not. Dad—she says GOD'S my father!" Whereupon the entire train burst into a laughter that lasted until the next station. My father, red about the ears, made a mental note to speak to the vocal one, as well as the budding catechist next to him.

What with one thing and another, the trip could take two and one half hours, and we would find Grandma at the other end of it in a state which might be described as less than joyous at the sight of seven green children trickling up her walk led by her poor son, obviously in a state of collapse. A bountiful dinner, long moribund on the stove, would be restored to a semblance of its former splendor. We would attempt to eat, with Grandma urging us on, and our protesting stomachs wanly refusing all but the daintiest morsel.

Occasionally, Grandma would invite two or three of us for a more prolonged visit just to reassure herself that we actually enjoyed good health. We loved that. Grandma had a houseful of interesting treasures. First in our affection, after Grandpa, of course, was a little canary named Sweet William. This was the first bird any of us became intimately acquainted with. Grandma had a tiny white bathtub for Sweet William, and the highlight of the visit came when Grandma prepared his bath. She set about it with a ritual of preparation that made the ablutions of Louis the Fourteenth look like a dip in the ole swimming hole.

First, we had to eliminate from the entire house any suggestion of drafts. We children would run about closing windows and transoms, and Grandma would light the oven if the kitchen registered less than ninety degrees on the little thermometer over the sink. Then the kitchen table was padded with newspaper, over which snowy white towels were laid. Grandma would fill the tiny tub with warm water, and place a red marble in it to attract his attention. While we sat in solemn silence around the table, breathless in anticipation, Grandma would extend a finger into the cage, and lo! the wondrous little yellow bird would hop onto it. Goggle-eyed, we would follow Grandma's progress across the kitchen, as she held the precious Sweet William, crooning soft little words to him all the while. Gently she would set him down on the snowy towel. Holding a finger to her lips, Grandma would caution us to a deeper stillness, and in this trancelike quiet the lovely Sweet William would grow confident and begin to waltz about, pecking at loose threads here and there, and turning his bright head to peer at us. Reassured of our hypnotic state, he would hop into the tub, and while we gasped and clutched our mouths in joy, he would splash about in a caricature of bathing. Spreading his wings, he would sluice his back, dousing the surrounding area with water, and chirping merrily.

When he was done, he would hop out, and Grandma would pick him up in a piece of soft flannel and gently dry his feathers. Then she would release him for the final feather arrangement he himself preferred, while she filled his seed and water cups and put fresh paper and gravel in the cage. This done, he would be returned to the cage once more, where the warmth and exercise finally overcame him, and he would duck his head under a wing to sleep.

Grandma had charming toys at her house; things my father and aunt had grown up with, and which she had carefully preserved: a little black wrought-iron stove, with miniature pots and pans; a doll carriage of the cherished coach style, complete with a beautiful old-fashioned doll; a French bed-doll done up in satin hoop skirts, like Marie Antoinette with powdered wig and dainty black high-heeled shoes; a boy soldier-doll (Confederate); but best of all, the Japanese garden.

This was a water toy, and I never again saw its equal for grace and charm. Grandma would cut an apple into segments and float them in water in a low, wide Japanese bowl. Then she would remove from their box exquisite little bisque Japanese pieces, each with a metal pin affixed to the base so that it could be inserted in the floating apple bits.

When all were in place, we saw before us a little Japanese village with a bridge and tiny people, all of whom could be moved at will by merely touching them with a little stick. It was hard for me, years later, to reconcile the stories of brutal Japanese soldiers with what I had learned of Japan from that exquisitely fragile miniature Japanese town.

The South Side, in those days, was the only place in Chicago where the Negroes lived. Two blocks from Grandma's house was the beginning of their neighborhood, and we loved to walk there. Wisely refraining from mentioning this to Grandma, who had an indefinable mental block about these excursions, we would walk slowly down the streets with the awe and appreciation of tourists. For the South Side Negroes had revolutionary notions about the area known as the front lawn. On Grandma's block, and all the blocks we knew as children, the idea of the front lawn was a sacred green patch, divided by sidewalk, upon whose bosom snow might have lain, but never a child's foot. There were exceptions, of course—if a ball you were playing with landed there, you might scan the windows of the house anxiously for possible lookouts, and hurriedly retrieve it. If the lawn-owner were resting on his porch swing, you asked him first if you might please get your ball, but more often than not, he would descend the stairs in silence, gingerly enter the Holy of Holies alone, and toss your ball back to you himself. As I say, the front lawn was sacred.

But the Negroes grew flowers in their front lawn. Their blocks were gay with sunflowers, zinnias, poppies, four-o'clocks, enormous cannas, and flowering shrubs. The porches always had flower boxes spilling over with petunias and fern. Though the colors ran riot, they never clashed.

Little Negro girls always wore hair ribbons, and seemed to favor yellow and pink dresses. I cannot recall ever seeing a dirty child or an angry adult there. The people we met were smiling, soft-spoken, and gentle, and I made one or two friendships among the little girls. We could never figure out Grandma's reluctance to have them come and play in her yard. She would become strangely embarrassed and tell us that the neighbors might not like it. Looking back now, I know with sadness the strains and pressures of that situation, and understand Grandma. I wish fervently Grandma had understood the Negroes two blocks down.

The South Side held the only gangster I ever saw. He was a minor bootlegger who lived a few doors away from my Aunt Marguerite, much to her consternation. Her concern appeared justified, inasmuch as he had enemies and all the bungalows on my aunt's block were identical. One night some of these displeased gentlemen passed the 8100 block, and pumped eighteen bullets into the grand piano of the people who lived next door to their intended victim.

The bootlegger had a magnificent front lawn. It was creeping bent grass, then relatively new to Chicago. My Uncle Bill sold us on the story that it was artificial grass which was rolled up each winter and stored in the basement. We longed to get close enough to have a good look at it, but a rather ugly looking gentleman maintained a twenty-four hour vigilance over the house and its environs, and we never got the chance.

My Father and the City of Chicago

My father is an idealist. He was born in a city whose very name raises eyebrows around the globe, but when he pronounces the word "Chicago," there is a ring in his voice that sounds as though he said "Olympus."

He is not hoodwinked, nor is he unknowing. An employee of the city of Chicago for forty years in the fastness of City Hall can hardly be said to be ignorant of the ways of the city. My father is simply a man of insight. He sees beyond the gaudy, crusty shell to the magnificent city Chicago is destined to be. After all, he will tell you, it is merely a question of emphasis.

Historically, my father's reckoning of Chicago's greatness begins with Father Marquette, sifts into the tragedy of Fort Dearborn, and gains a mounting crescendo of railroad development, business opportunities, and infant universities. Renewed, rather than destroyed by the Great Fire, my father's city rolls on to the marbled grace of the Columbian Exposition, the landscaped shore of our inland sea, the vast network of parks spread between quiet, decent neighborhoods, the droning highways reaching outward from the Loop to all corners of the city: these are the symbols of its greatness. The color and glamor of the little national sections where Mexicans, Chinese, and Greeks begin anew the urbanization that the Irish, German, Italians, and Poles learned before them, the vast churning mixture of peoples, this is my father's city. Al Capone and the rest of the ugliness of the twenties is an unfortunate footnote to the tale as far as my father is concerned.

To this day I never emerge from the city heat to the wide, gracious green shore of Lake Michigan without knowing again a joy that stretches back to childhood. For we believed that Lake Michigan, the Outer Drive, our museums, parks, public buildings, and forest preserves were the most beautiful part of the universe. My father

told us this himself, and he spoke with such conviction that no one could ever doubt his sincerity.

"Take a look at that lake!" he would tell us, waving his arm in a spacious arc, "there isn't a more beautiful lake in the world!" And then he would turn from the beach and point to the glittering row of skyscrapers behind us and add:

"Nowhere on earth is there a skyline like ours!"

My father not only loved Chicago, he spent most of his spare time herding us through its streets. There were seven of us, and I sometimes wonder at the quiet heroism of a man who was willing to spend his Sunday afternoons boarding streetcars, transferring on buses, and tending to the inevitable mishaps and illness incurred by seven children, in order to show us the Art Institute's newest exhibit, the Natural History Museum, or, on really long rides, the Museum of Science and Industry.

I still wander back to these beloved places. El Greco's "Assumption" still soars queenlike over the same room at the Art Institute; the Colleen Moore Doll House still casts the enchanting thrall of fairyland over the hearts of little girls. I take my children excursioning, but under vastly more comfortable conditions than my father did.

Dad had pioneering blood. We lived on the far northwest side of the city, and when Dad's vacation came, it meant two weeks of almost daily travel to the beach. The Addison bus, with its policy of closed windows and pungent gas fumes, was the scene of many highly embarrassing scenes, necessitating hurried exits from the bus, and a subsequent repayment of fares for all when the afflicted member had been restored to bloom. Dad often remarked after particularly rocky rides that it would have been much cheaper to go by cab.

Emerging at length at Oak Street, we would head for a fruit store where Dad would buy a shopping bag full of provender; then, armed with towels, beach bags, an inner tube, fodder, and bottles of sun-tan lotion, we would take our lives in our hands and shoot across Michigan Avenue, climb out of our clothing (having prudently worn our

bathing suits underneath), and joyfully dash into the lake. Dad couldn't swim, and I sometimes wonder what would have happened if one of us had succumbed to an undertow or cramps, but it just never came up. He would sit there in an island of beach bags and shoes and watch benignly; counting us frequently, smearing lotion on anyone incautious enough to get close, and smoking cigars.

Through some alchemy, known only to him, Dad always knew when it was five o'clock and time to go home. This was the only sour note in the day. For we invariably found ourselves boarding buses with our sandy tire and sandy towels and wet suits (under our clothing) right at the rush hour when everyone was returning home from work, tired, and not too eager to sit near seven damp and slightly scorched children. But Dad saw us through with a jovial patience I marvel at. Just the thought of trying to do that now wearies me.

Wintertime held its own white magic; Dad taught us to ice skate on the pond at Garfield Park. The boathouse at the rear of the field building was converted into a wooden-floored skating shelter in wintertime; a potbellied stove provided heat for the frozen ones, and a little concession stand sold candy and soft drinks. Long benches were the only furniture provided, and we would line up on these, while Dad patiently laced each skate, tightened the straps, and sent us out on the ice one at a time. When the last one had been launched, Dad would don his own skates and sail out grandly. He was a fine skater, and we marveled at the strength of his ankles. Ours were always at twenty-degree angles. He would circle about, helping one or another of us, rescuing fallen ones, and checking on mittens and scarves.

Mother seldom accompanied us on these athletic jousts; the times we were away from the house provided the only relaxation she found in those early years. But on Sunday afternoons she frequently accompanied us to the Garfield Park Conservatory to see the flower shows. We loved the conservatory; particularly the room where the ferns and rubber plants grew. There was a tropical moisture here amid the exotic growth, and Tom and I would pretend to be on a safari through some secret South American jungle. Orchids grew here in profusion; the first I ever saw.

When I visit the conservatory now I am more delighted with the visitors than the flowers. Old people come here, their faces lit with the recollection of other gardens. Invalids in wheel chairs are propelled slowly down the lush paths of banked, chromatically staged bouquets, and the happiness in their faces is better than the rarest bloom. But when we were young we saw none of this. We ran on ahead, skipping over the little streams of water, and pointing gleefully at the goldfish. My father told us that this conservatory was the largest in the country; Chicago's would be.

When I went back to see the flower show recently, I found that the main room of the Garfield Park Conservatory had been done over in fiber glass and all the vegetation I knew so well as a child had been replaced with new stock. It will be growing for another forty years, I suppose, and my children were entranced. But I felt like Alice after she took the wrong pill: twenty feet high. All the banana trees and palms seemed to have shrunk.

Brookfield Zoo, with its magnificent vistas and its concept of cageless housing of animals in a luxurious natural setting, had not been completed when we first went zoo-ing together. Lincoln Park Zoo, home of Bushman, the gorilla, was a favorite haunt of every Chicago child. The larger, fiercer animals had little appeal for me; it was the tiny rabbit village that drew me. Quaint little houses, every one different, were hutches for the rabbit population there, and I used to stand by the fence for long periods of time looking at the elderly hares like old men sitting in doorways or peering out the windows. Cottontailed bunnies hopped about between the houses like children playing on lawns. Bushman held the prime place with my brothers, though. He was a gorilla of unusual intelligence and size, and could be made to do tricks. Admiring crowds gathered before his cage when the keeper put him through his routine. As the years went on, his personality became crotchety, and he was finally considered dangerous. His death made the headlines, and he may be seen today, restored to a lifelike pose, glaring out at the children from behind a case in the Natural History Museum.

My father was vastly proud of the Chicago Water Department. Part of his enjoyment of the lake stemmed from the fact that it provided Chicago with the purest and least expensive water in the world. I was visiting pumping stations when I was four years old. The romance of the water tower left standing in the wake of the Great Fire unfolded to me before I was six. Whenever he could arrange it through friends, Dad would take us out to visit the cribs [water intake stations] in the lake to watch the operation from there. Though it was on these trips that we discovered that car and bus sickness were nothing compared to the horrors of seasickness, we found these trips informative and exhilarating. I can even remember being dressed in miner's clothing, including hip boots, exploring a new sewer project with my father.

We made countless pilgrimages to the airport, Tribune Tower, and Michigan Avenue, and when the Grant Park concerts began, my father's love for Chicago became a paean of praise. For him, the city was a vast book of knowledge and beauty, free for the taking, and to share it with his children was as natural as breathing.

When we were older, and became aware that not everyone loved Chicago as we did, we were puzzled, and asked my father about it. Dad blamed the newspapers. He said that every city on earth had its share of evil men and stealthy deeds, but that they seldom broadcast these facts. Chicago papers, or some of them, seemed waiting for something to happen so they could feature it as front page news.

"Most of the criminals who have made Chicago infamous were not even born here," Dad said. "They're from New York, or little hick towns out West. They come to Chicago and foul our city with their crimes, and our newspapers play it up big to sell papers." He regarded this a gross betrayal of the public trust, and certain newspapers were banned in our home as a result of their wild-eyed reporting of the seamy side of the city.

Chicago, to my parents, was their homeland; their birthplace. They had a love for the city which grew out of the Irish tendency to remember with pride and affection the place of their birth. For them, it was a community of churches (largest Catholic diocese in the world), fine educational institutions (site of the universities of Chicago and Illinois and of Loyola, Northwestern, and De Paul universities), and a treasury of cultural opportunities for rich and poor alike.

The land of promise it must have seemed to their fore-bears, fresh from the green hills of Dubuque and the little river town of Moline, was still verdant for my mother and father. The city rewarded their trust by unfolding it's best for them, always.

I drove along the lake front again today. It sparkled blue and crystal beside the city, and the wide expanse of green parks held the beauty I first knew as a child. I have learned to be grateful for the privilege of having grown up in Chicago. It *is* the most wonderful city in the world. My gratitude is beyond telling to the father who had the vision and love to point it out to me.

The Planetarium

A slim green arm reaches out into the sparkling waters of Lake Michigan; a peninsula strategically placed by the city fathers, and ornamented with a single monument to science: the Adler Planetarium. And Chicagoans go to the planetarium like pilgrims. It is our mecca; our dark Taj Mahal. When life becomes too tangled, or the city too steamingly humid, or our souls long to be nearer heaven, we go to the planetarium. Of course, no one ever goes inside. "Going to the planetarium" means just that. We go to it; never into it.

The setting is impressively grandiose. Central roads down the middle of the peninsula lead to the great domed building itself. But green lawns to either side stretch temptingly down to the concreted lake edge on the left, and on the right, to a minuscule airport sandwiched between a toy harbor and more lake. Few on that straight and narrow path manage to withstand the distractions along the way, but wander down to the water. Foreign students actually go inside, of course, and Middle Western tourists conscientiously "seeing Chicago." One is always aware, from a comfortably prone position on the sloping lawn, that there is a trickle of horn-rimmed Japanese just leaving, their spectacles and camera lenses gleaming in the sun. And there is always that delightful contingent of newly arrived visitors shepherding a gaggle of dark-skinned children, all dressed up in ruffled, starched clothing they are trying desperately to keep clean. The father

of this family is always wearing a business suit and a straw hat. This clearly separates him from the Chicago populace, which tends to casual clothing for the lake front. The mother is wearing a wrinkled suit and is hatted, gloved, and worried about whether there is a public rest room in the planetarium, since the youngest has drunk heavily of pop.

Sunday afternoons bring the young people, the tourists, and the sailors from Great Lakes. Sailors always travel in threes for some reason, and they amble along, looking at the girls, or congregate along the worn concrete steps to watch the small-craft owners struggle with new boats. Sailboats dipping in and out of the harbor, flirting along the peninsula's edge, suddenly strike bravely off for Milwaukee or St. Joe across the lake. Fiber glass cabin cruisers, filled with blonde young things in clothes from Saks, glide by, waving indiscriminately at persons along the shore.

But it is the weekday dusk that reveals the essence of "going to the planetarium." In the late afternoon, when the work of the day is over, come the fishermen. Negroes from the teaming West Side neighborhoods, carrying dinner in boxes and mysterious fishing gear, stream silently down along the edge of the shore line and prepare for the evening's sport. A labyrinth of line and hook is strung out with infinite care and left to be supported by bobbers. The owner of the gear stretches out on the concrete, drinks his coffee, and munches sandwiches, and views his enterprise with seemingly casual interest. Now and then he arises to inspect the hooks to see whether the bait has been nibbled, and then returns to his position near the food. Perhaps some day a really big fish will bite; a large fish that will provide a good dinner. Meanwhile

the little perch will do. For has he not found something
better than fish? Is there not reward enough in this comfortable perspective far from the crowded city streets,
with the majestic skyline to contemplate, the breezes
heady as wine, the spanking white sails and the sky opening up its daily drama of cloud-spires and scudding sun-
tipped nimbi as prelude to the slowly drawing velvet of
the night?

Myriad little Negro boys race up and down the peninsula. Shouting indistinguishably to one another, they
wrestle in the grass with high glee. They all seem eleven
years old; wiry and happy. One seldom sees little Negro
girls there; perhaps only the boys have bikes.

And the lovers, the ever-present lovers! When a girl and
boy go to the planetarium they are really in love. For
there is no real privacy here, only beauty and wind and
water. But the girls, with their hair blown to more natural
state by the wind, and their summer dresses whipped
about, seem more feminine somehow; and the boys,
bronze-armed in light sport shirts, more protective and
masculine. They walk along the water's edge together, the
boys assisting the girls over the more dangerous spots.
Lifting their heads high to the breeze, they point to the
Grecian-templed museum across the drive beyond, and
recall the trips they took with parents when they were
children. They smile at the remembrance of the visits to
the aquarium and vow that their children will share all
of this. They believe they are alone on the peninsula.
Afterward they will be unable to recall whether or not
the shore was crowded. There were just the two of them,
with the sky, the blue water, and later the stars over the
glittering skyline.

Two things I must do before I die: learn to sail a boat
and go inside the planetarium.

Through the Nose

There is every indication that the movies, in addition to being better than ever, wider than ever, and deeper than ever, are now going to smell more than ever before. Hollywood has recently announced the flowering of a new concept in movie making, imaginatively christened "Smella-vision." What at first glance seems to be a rather terse comment on TV, turns out to be a system whereby odor, locked into the movie film, will be detected by the viewers by means of a system of ducts cunningly placed around the theater. Just how this will be accomplished is somewhat secret at present, and even after it is explained, will remain a secret still to me. My mind balks at scientific explanations. But there are several phases of this new marvel which are stunningly clear. For one thing, the screen credits will have to be even longer than they are at present, to make room for the proper obeisance to the talented odors emanating from the screen.

The next fact is obvious. Theater ventilation can no longer be achieved simply with Air-Wick. The concerto of aroma from a single afternoon's feature will raise this aspect of theater-keeping to titanic heights. Outdoor theaters may have the edge here. Tents may even be used again, with roll-up sides to let in God's fresh air. At any rate, something will have to be done. The whole dramatic impact of a love scene would be entirely ruined if preceding it had been some action involving, say, a cattle roundup. And consider the sabotage done a homey

living-room scene with the pungent hospital antiseptic of the previous scene still wafting about the collective nose.

Long ago, when Superman and I were young, we spent our Saturday afternoons together at the Patio. This picture palace was located two blocks from home; it was run by a Mr. Mitchell, one of the few people we knew who drove a Cadillac. My father used to claim he had bought this car for Mr. Mitchell. There were seven of us, and after all, seven dimes a week, over a period of years, might have gone a long way toward the purchase of this status symbol. We used to stand in line outside the Patio a full forty minutes on a Saturday afternoon, awaiting the magical moment when Mr. Mitchell would open the doors.

There was plenty to do—chat with our confreres, read all the coming attractions, and speculate on the probable outcome of the last episode of the serial, in which Superman had been apparently blown to bits in a mining shack. Finally the doors would open; we would all give our dimes to Mrs. Mitchell (my father said they were working on a mink coat next) and then go in and stay for two shows. Anyone who left after one show was either sick or due to go to a party. The sick theory was easily documented. I used to have a headache every Saturday afternoon. I learned to bring my own aspirin to the movies.

About halfway through each show, Herbie Schultz, the butcher's son, who was employed as an usher, would walk down the aisle with a bottle of "Apple Blossom" cologne with a long dangling atomizer on it. Systematically spraying all four aisles, he would create an unforgettable effluvium, concocted of equal parts of perfume, popcorn, and leather jackets, which we found delightful.

The Saturday matinee was always crowded because the

children of the neighborhood met there to visit, trade baseball cards, check on homework, and catch up on the latest news, such as, who had been sent to the Superior's office on Friday, and why. It was our clubhouse. Uninformed adults who were foolish enough to attend the movies for Saturday afternoon's soiree were apt to be beaned by flying popcorn boxes, or deafened by the combined din of the screen's blazing six-guns and the audience participation.

Father Lord once took us, I remember. He walked into that bedlam with seven kids in tow, but when the lights went on (to allow the starving a chance to revive themselves at the popcorn counter) he found himself alone. We were all visiting friends up and down the aisles.

One or two adults, trapped into taking young relatives to the afternoon serial might be seen staggering toward the exits, clutching their throats and wiping tears from their eyes. This was passed off as further evidence of adult peculiarity. It was several years later, when a chance invitation took me to another theater and I emerged without the usual headache, that the possible connection with Herbie's atomizer dawned on me. Little did I realize however, that Herbie Schultz was the herald of an age when smell would arise not only from an atomizer but from the very walls of the theater itself.

In those pre-Legion of Decency days, Mother and Dad saw a lot of movies. They had to, in order to know whether or not they were fit for our young eyes. They could have saved themselves a lot of trouble, had they known how fleeting was our attention to the screen. Love scenes were roundly and unanimously booed. Scenes of tenderness and sentimental moments were loudly commented upon, adversely; so that whatever impression was intended by Hollywood was seriously altered by Chicago. We lived only for the fleeting moments of the Selected Short Subjects and the Previews of Coming Attractions.

The Selected Short Subjects always contained a Donald Duck or Mickey Mouse cartoon, a little gem of comedy starring Benchley or Laurel and Hardy; a sportsreel (hurray!) a newsreel (boos), and a travelogue. Sometimes there would be a sing-a-long with a bouncing white ball, and organ accompaniment from the pit. But the serial—that was the great thing. It was this that lured us back week after week, month after month, to follow the precarious adventures of a hero who, despite a penchant for getting into impossible situations each week, redeemed himself just in the nick of time the following week.

The Previews, telling of delights to come, were signals for wholesale planning for the following Saturday. As Saturday's selection was announced, a voice in the balcony would call:

"Hey, Dave, are you going to come next week?" Dave, in the third row, would yell back:

"Nah, it looks crummy." But Harry, Joe, and Pete would check out as among those planning to attend, while the distraught Herbie flashed his futile light around trying to find the vocal culprits.

Smellavision appears to me replete with fresh problems and concerns. Hollywood may be rushing barefoot into new thickets. They'll need whole new departments for olfactory research. Specialists will have to be hired to decide questions like "What does it smell like on the moon?" which might well involve the expense of a trip to outer space. Dependence on specialists will further raise the prices of admission, contributing to inflation, and gluing

John Q more firmly to his television set, soothed only by the redolence of his beer. Dollar for dollar, Herbie and his atomizer would be cheaper. The last time I visited the dime store, "Apple Blossom" cologne was still selling big, and for all I know Herbie may still be available. It wasn't *that* long ago.

Books

Much has been written, in this highly literate country, on why Johnnie can't read. Theories range from incorrect teaching methods to prenatal trauma, with TV and comic books ranking high as villains. I have a theory of my own, which I offer with confidence born of the realization that this is my book. "Johnnie," the archetype of our six-to-ten-year-old population, is a highly imitative youngster. I believe Johnnie can't read because he has never had the experience of seeing his elders read for sheer enjoyment.

Father scans the morning headlines with keen displeasure, and scowls mightily at them. Mother reads the mail impatiently, and dumps most of it into the wastebasket, after burying the unwelcome bills in the desk drawer.

Johnnie is being taught the mechanics of reading along with every other youngster in the school system. He is also being taught, through those most persuasive teachers, his parents, that reading at best is a humdrum exercise, which he must endure so that he will pass third grade. He sees little evidence that it can be a thoroughly rewarding experience, and loses, thereby, the only incentive which will carry him through the difficulties ahead.

My mother and father produced seven youngsters with a profound allergy to mathematics, but they had no Johnnies-who-can't-read. The reason was simple. From the time we were old enough to get about the house on two legs we were taught that books were precious things.

We were not permitted to mistreat books, and we would
have no more dog-eared one of my father's books than
we would have carved our initials in the table tops. We
had coloring books galore. These were decorated, torn,
masticated, as the spirit moved us. But a book—and to
our minds this was identified as a treasure bound in a hard
cover, filled with incomprehensible words which our
parents somehow loved—a book was to be handled
gently, with clean hands, and with a respect that was
felt rather than spoken.

Our evenings in those early childhood days were
centered about a long library table lit by a brass reading
lamp with a colored glass shade. Mother and Dad sat near
it, quietly reading, and we children sat under it, playing
the many games evoked by the possibilities of a cavelike
structure in a safe, warm room. And as soon as there was
the slightest interest on our part, my father began the
nightly practice of reading aloud to us. This was something he loved. Through these books he could share with
us the stories he had enjoyed; through these books he

bridged for us the time gap which lay between his generation and ours.

His first ventures in this regard were the Father Finn
books. I tried to read them recently, and found them
sadly dated. But when I was a little girl, I loved them all.
We also became familiar with Phil the Fiddler, Paul the
Peddler, and the multitude of fascinating personages who
made good in the world of Horatio Alger. One of Dad's
early stories, a Father Finn tale called *His First And Last
Appearance*, I have never forgotten. It concerned a boy
with a beautiful singing voice, and the author included
the words of the Christmas carol "O Holy Night," which
I didn't actually hear—musically, that is—until about five
years later when Sister M. Edward taught it to us at
Christmas time. I shall never forget the thrill of hearing
the words I had loved so long set to music. It is still my
favorite Christmas song.

Dad never stopped to explain words we didn't understand and it never occurred to us to ask him. We took it
for granted that in this higher atmosphere of pleasure,
there was not only exultation and joy, but mystery. Much
of what my father read to us fell into that mysterious
category. My mother, a teacher, eyed us with some concern when she would come in and find Dad stretched out
on the floor with *Oliver Twist* and three children, aged
seven, five, and three, sitting around him in a state of
heavy-lidded torpor.

"George," she would protest, "for heaven's sake let
these children go to bed! It's past nine, and they don't
understand a word of what you're reading anyway."

But we were discovering a world of enjoyment which
was artlessly compounded of our father's time, a sense
of happy security, a book which had been written by a

master craftsman and read with relish and obvious pleasure by our greatest teacher. At the age of eleven, I picked up the book myself, and found out what Dad had been reading about. I found there the world he had charted for us years before.

Our first trips to the library were adventures I have never forgotten. We lived some eight blocks from the nearest branch of the Chicago Public Library system, and since our summer chores included minding the smaller children, Tom and I would pull them in a coaster wagon. We took turns lugging and lifting them up and down curbs. When at length we arrived at the library, our first concern was to lift Virginia and Rosemary up to the drinking fountain, and locate the washroom. Then we would herd them in on tiptoe to the children's room, seat them at the low, inviting tables, and place picture books in front of them. We two elders were then free to browse through the stacks to find the treasures we would take home with us.

The libraries had a happy policy of allowing borrowers to take as many as fourteen books home for vacation

reading. Tom and I both gathered our full quota, as well
as the baby books for Virginia and Rosemary. And what
finds there were! Tom was entranced with the section
mapped out for the boys, and read adventure stories of
pirates and cowboys. I was determined to read every book
in the girl's section, as well as the titles I recognized from
my parents' recommended list. It's a wonder I didn't go
blind. Five books a week were nothing for me, and I had
soon cut a wide swathe through the children's shelves.
At the age of twelve I was sweating it out with Dickens,
chuckling through Tarkington, and roaring at Wodehouse,
who became a hot favorite with the entire family.

We would sit on the front steps for hours, reading our
books, and pestering one another by reading the choice
bits aloud. Wodehouse fans have favorite passages in
that zany world of the Drones Club and white-spatted
younger sons. My favorite concerned the prize giving at
the Market-Snodsberry School for Boys, during which
Gussie Finknoodle had been fortified by a hooker by
each of his friends in turn, all unknown to one another,
until the prize-giving program found him highly inebri-
ated, and equal to the occasion at last. He tacked down
to the edge of the stage, smiling and snapping his braces,
to bestow the scripture prize on young Smith. The dia-
logue went something like:

"And what is your name, my fine young man?"

"Sir, Smith, sir."

"Smith, eh? How old are you, Smith?"

"Sir, eleven, sir."

"Married, Smith?"

"Sir, no sir."

"Get married, Smith! It's the only life!"

This exchange fractured me, and still does. The curious

thing is, it was through the reading aloud of this passage
that I discovered for the first time that everyone does not
agree on what constitutes humor. Much to my amazement,
I found that there were people in the world who did
not respond to Wodehouse. They seemed normal in every
respect, were kind to children and dogs and so on, but
Wodehouse left them cold. It was a valuable lesson in
tolerance for me; but I still approach such people with
wariness. Not to love Wodehouse! Or to miss the happy
folly of Stephen Potter! To be deaf to the gentle whimsey
of Thurber, or the wacky verbosity of Perelman. Ah
well, it takes all kinds!

This love of reading, implanted at a tender age by my
parents, has led me into adventures more truly fruitful
than any of my formal schooling. Following my father's
habit of trying to uncover, by a program of reading, all
the facts pertinent to any individual subject, I decided to
try to read my way through the Great Books list. I should
have joined a group of people, I suppose, and done it in
the approved manner. But I had three young children at
home, and very little spare time, so I got the list, and
went off to the library to get the books. I was led that day
down a trail of learning that is still stretching out before
my weakening eyes. For, though Adler and Hutchins had
placed the Bible about three or four down on the list, I
decided that it certainly predated any other work as far
as I was concerned, and I began with the Bible.

Mortimer Adler had written a tome called *How To
Read A Book*, which insisted that the only proper way was
to read it three times. I began the pilgrim's progress
through the Bible—three times. It took me months on end.
I would throw a load of clothes in the washing machine,
and read a chapter of Leviticus; do the dishes and read

another, and so on. I developed an undeserved reputation for piety within my family; whenever any of my brothers or sisters came to visit, there was I, reading the Good Book.

Having begun as an intellectual exercise, I soon realized that I was robbing myself of indulgences by not reading this holy book with a purposeful intention; I began each reading with the prayer at the beginning of the Bible. At length the task was ended. But by this time I was a different person. I had developed an appetite for reading which would nourish my spirit and encourage it to growth.

This discovery led me to Father John Hardon, a Jesuit teacher of theology at West Baden College in Indiana. Father gave me a bibliography to guide my reading, one he had drawn up for the teaching of seminarians. For the next three years I paddled about in a sea of books. They opened up a new world for me, and are responsible for whatever progress I have made since that time. I became acquainted with the saints, not through the little stories from school, but through their own works. Their dynamic and powerful words rang in my heart with a force I shall never forget. St. Theresa of Avila, St. John of the Cross, and St. Ignatius; masters of the spiritual life, spoke to me, as well as Ferdinand Prat, Walter Farrell, M. C. D'Arcy, C. C. Martindale, Gerald Vann, Alban Goodier, Giuseppi Ricciotti, Jean Daniélou, Eugene Boylan, Vincent McNabb, Emanuel Suhard, John T. Ellis, Ronald Knox, and Jacques Maritain. The vast new horizons of the mind which these men unlocked are still largely unexplored terrain to me. But I know where my spirit will go adventuring whenever it has the opportunity. The allure of the morning paper is forgotten.

Nothing is as stale as yesterday's news; nothing more new and pertinent than the fruits of the contemplation of these great men.

Time and *America* are my weekly diet of comment, representing the secular and the Catholic with equal force. But Father Hardon's bibliography has replaced the Great Books program for me. It will take me a lifetime to get through it all, and if it inspires something approaching virtue at the end of the trail it will prove more valuable than all the wealth of human knowledge man has gathered.

There is evidence that the family penchant for learning through reading has been passed on to the present generation. My own children love to read, and show promise of continuing beyond the childhood stage. My little niece, Carolyn, read me a little treatise on the state of Illinois the other day. She filled me in on the cogent facts about our state flower, motto, seal, etc., and I was greatly impressed.

"Carolyn," I asked her, "do you ever read fairy tales?"

She shook her pigtails vigorously and wrinkled up her little freckled nose.

"I only like true things," she stated, virtuously. Carolyn is seven.

She has a way of taking statements in a literal manner that is sometimes disconcerting. Last year she floored her mother by announcing at dinner that her sister in school had a baby. My sister Loretta was stunned, but rallied sufficiently to cover her dismay with a quiet explanation.

"No, darling. Sisters don't get married. They never have children." Carolyn was insistent.

"My sister has a little girl—she told me she did." Loretta knew when she was licked.

"All right, dear; what did sister say?"

"Sister said, 'Carolyn dear, you remind me so much of a little girl I had last year!'" Loretta explained what Sister meant by that, mentally thanking her stars that she had had the opportunity of getting at the core of the confusion before Carolyn had spread her tale around the neighborhood.

Carolyn could read before she started kindergarten. She has read all the seventh and eighth grade books at school. Any day now, I expect to find Carolyn and Grandpa lying on the rug together, with *Oliver Twist*. She's just about the right age for it.

Our Lady of Angels

When I read today of the hue and cry over prayers in the public schools, and the final crowning idiocy of a lady somewhere in the East who has begun suit to eliminate the stanza of "The Star-Spangled Banner" which refers to our motto "In God We Trust," I thank again the parents who cared so much for me that they were willing to pay for a Catholic education.

It is terrifying to me that an American woman should have descended so far from the spirit of the early settlers of this country that she should be seeking to eliminate the very name of God from our national anthem. Mother and Dad were cut from different cloth. They educated seven children through Catholic schools. There were no cars, nor summer vacation trips, nor luxuries of any kind other than the happy home they so freely gave us. But they presented us with the priceless gift that we are building our lives on: a way of thought and action calculated to help us become good citizens of America, and of that other Kingdom not of this world.

No one removed from the actual budget-jockeying necessary to the task can possibly appreciate what it means for a middle-class family to remain faithful to the ideal of a Catholic education for their youngsters. The cost of living today is at an all-time high. Parents of public school children wring their hands over tax increases, food costs, and mounting clothing bills. Catholic parents have all of these to contend with, and keep their arms and hearts open to an open-end family whose size is determined by Providence instead of Dow-Jones averages. They send these children on to Catholic schools.

During my high school years, I was enrolled at Our Lady of Angels Academy, in Clinton, Iowa, where my cousins also attended school. It was a small boarding academy, where much stress was placed on "being a lady."

OLA was situated on a hill. The buildings were old, but well cared for. There was a little farmyard off to one side where Sister M. Hubert kept a flock of chickens. The façades of the buildings, impressively Georgian, overlooked a sloping driveway lined with giant trees, and a little park which honored St. Joseph with a white marble statue. A stream wound through the grounds, crossed at intervals by rustic bridges from which we could watch the tadpoles and polliwogs wriggling about in the Mississippi waters, which sidetracked through the campus grounds. The minim school was fronted with a little wooden patio where chairs were placed for resting, and from which one had a lovely view of trees, umbrellaed tables, the toboggan slope, and the cinder path that led to the grotto of Our Lady.

Inside the school, there prevailed the aroma of fresh wax and incense from the chapel, that seems a hallmark of every sisters' school I have ever entered; the fragrance of cleanliness and order, which speaks of gentlewomen. The sisters, dear faces framed in white and enshrined in memory's sweetest corridors, were the school. It was they who gave it life and beauty and warmth; it was they who sparked the classes with keen intelligence and equally keen wit, and made learning an interesting and rewarding experience.

Sister Mary St. Matthew, who had the third year home

room during my first year at OLA, became my closest friend. Sister was about five foot four, with very square shoulders, and the poise of a queen. Eyes of blue-violet pierced the most carefully prepared mask and found the truth beyond. Her aristocratic voice, unforgettable in anger, was equally unforgettable reading poetry, so that her third and fourth year classes in English were scenes of fire and ice. We *had* to love literature; Matty made it clear that not to love the sweep and splendor of great writing was somehow disgraceful and unworthy of Catholic young women. She reigned supreme over our minds during those two crucial years, imbedding a taste for the true and the beautiful that conquered our adolescent vacillations and found dwelling places in our feminine souls. Her handwriting, small and superb like herself, crawled all over our efforts at composition like a stream of mercury, seeking dangling participles, daggering the misspelled word, spearing the inert punctuation, and, happily, praising a well-turned phrase.

Her position as dean cast her in many roles besides that of teacher. Saturday afternoon would find Sister organizing hikes out to Eagle Point Park, or descending upon our lockers and bureaus with the zeal of a Marine sergeant, noting disorder and signs of bad housekeeping. The offenders were instantly punished with campusing or demerits; but Sister could never stay displeased with anyone for any length of time. The girl who had been pilloried for having neglected to change the lining paper in her dresser drawers would find Sister seeking her out for a walk around the campus the next day.

Matty insisted on a great deal of exercise. She was an amazing basketball player, and she could whip anyone at tennis. It pained her to see me during those solemn occasions when the sophomores took on the seniors at basketball, hiding somewhere under the stacks of chairs with a book, instead of "getting out there and chasing the cobwebs out of your brain." Maude and I, who were inseparable in those boarding school days, would try to become scarce whenever Matty began organizing a game. Sometimes we managed to escape up to Maudie's room, which was at the remotest point from the gym; but inevitably the intrepid Matty would swoop down on us, knock the books from our nerveless fingers, and demand to know why we weren't in uniform like the rest of the class. Badgered, we would go and don the hated gym clothing, and enter the fray. Five minutes later, with tears of laughter running down her cheeks, she would haul us out of the game again, and command us to watch

from the sidelines so as not to ruin the game for the others. Those were painful sessions.

The entire enrollment of OLA seldom climbed above two hundred girls during any given year. Gracing the walls of the dormitory corridors were pictures of the graduating classes dating back to the school's founding in the late nineteenth century, when the diploma was given to an exclusive five or six. A careful perusal of those unknown faces, silently regarding us from the fixed positions of their posed portraits, was a favorite sport on Sunday afternoons. The history of women's dress and hair styling through the whole tortured period of emancipation was there on our walls. Some of the pictures were riotous; the particular favorites being the curtain-draped waves of the twenties. It is clearly poetic justice that Maudie and I are up there now, along with the other scoffers of those years, and are probably being subjected to the same kind of unrelenting scrutiny by the OLA girls of today.

I learned about physics and geometry at OLA. The sister who taught these mysteries was a charming personality who played the trumpet in her off hours, and regaled us with stories of her youth. We learned a great deal about dealing with boys from her, along with valuable suggestions about dress and deportment that girls today must go to finishing school to acquire. We also learned about the privilege of being a Catholic woman from these faithful brides of Christ.

Every day began with Mass, at 5:30 A.M. Evening prayers in chapel ended the day. Without any special exhortation that I can recall, we got the impression that our little chapel was the most important room in the entire school, since it was the home of our Divine Guest. Any hour we entered, we would find several sisters in the rear pews, and many of our classmates quietly kneeling in adoration. Sometimes, after exams, a girl might be crying—a low mark, a reprimand, or no mail from home that day takes on gigantic proportions in an all-girl school. But a little time in chapel made everyone feel better, and we soon came to make frequent visits part of our daily life. I miss many things about the past; none so keenly as that opportunity of actually living in a house where the Blessed Sacrament was reserved. It gave the serenity and peace to Our Lady of Angels that was so clearly reflected in the calm, lovely faces of our sisters.

Sister M. St. Matthew took every problem to God. I cannot imagine her ever crying over anything, however. I suspect Matty took her woes to God with characteristic queenliness of bearing. She was not above speaking sternly to the saints, I'm sure, in her determination that the Lord be advised of her particular cause at the moment. But once having stated the problem in clear, precise tones, and reverently demanding that the Lord give it His immediate consideration, Matty never looked back at it. She was absolutely certain that God had not only heard her prayer, but was taking care of it pronto. Whatever happened subsequently, it was clearly the holy will of God. This assurance and security was responsible for Sister's calm in the face of turmoil. No disaster, however terrifying, could move Matty from her position at the eye of the storm. Faith in her loving Father in heaven was her bulwark and staff.

Every Christmas since I left OLA twenty-four years ago, and every birthday as well, has brought charming little notes from Sister M. St. Matthew. She has been shifted into every corner of the country, but she has sailed through each parting and new beginning like the valiant woman she is. Recently I saw her again and found her in that particular condition of agelessness that seems part of a nun's hundredfold from God. Her skin is fresh and clear as a girl's; the wonderful eyes sparkle with fun; the mind still probes keenly after truth. I have never been able to figure out her exact age; I only know that I now am about ten years older than Matty in appearance. The square little shoulders know no droop; the habit hangs straight and proud from them. She lifts her head with the same imperial dignity; few famous beauties have managed to retain youthfulness with her success. It must be she is forever a favorite child in the house of a loving and indulgent Father.

One of the favorite indoor sports at OLA, particularly around exam time, was to feign illness. One of the sophomores became so adept at fainting in chapel that she could pass out practically at will, and she confided her secret to a few intimate friends: wet blotters inside her shoes. Vague feelings of headachy queasiness could be parlayed into double pneumonia if one knew how to go about it. Sister Mary Hubert, the infirmarian, could always be relied upon to put the aching shell to bed, for one afternoon at least. She dosed us with football pills (a powerful purge) and allowed us to rest in the infirmary. However, no radio or visitors or books were permitted to accompany the ailing one to sick bay, so that the catharsis, aided by sheer boredom, restored us to bloom by morning.

During one memorable flu scare, however, when the returning boarders arrived after the Christmas holidays, they were met at the front door by Sister M. Hubert, who administered large doses of football pills to everyone. She was taking no chances on our dragging illness into the sacred corridors. Sister forgot, apparently, what a

strain this procedure would put on the plumbing, as approximately one hundred and fifty football pills took action at the same moment about four hours later. This crisis proved the only time in school history that we were admitted to the sacrosanct and hidden area known as the nuns' quarters.

We belonged to the Sodality of Our Lady at OLA, in

those benighted days before you had to pass an intelligence test to get in. It was blandly assumed that every Catholic girl was material for the Sodality, and we held meetings and distributed good works and pamphlets, blissfully unaware that only a few years later the Sodality would go exclusive. Those meetings were wonderful to behold. Committees reported on every aspect of sodalist activity we could think of, and there was much worried discussion of the danger of communism. We read of the heroic work of the priests behind the scenes in Russia, keeping alive the faith of the people; we went en masse to the Summer School of Catholic Action in Chicago.

During one particularly lively discussion about whether we should send some reading material to the Mississippi State Prison, one of the girls in the back row screamed,

"A bat! There's a bat in here!" He had escaped from the infested cupola, I suppose, and was flying blindly about, darting helplessly over the heads of the screeching girls, and causing more pandemonium than an atomic bomb. The sister in charge, filled with a womanly valor, stood up and called us to order in quavering tones,

"Girls—listen to me, girls—it's all right . . . just cover your heads with your veils so it won't get into your hair!" And we all promptly turbaned our heads with our chapel veils, while Mildred Crisanti went after *die Fledermaus* with a broom. She finally brought him down on the stage, bowed in response to our frenzied applause, and then dispatched him in a bucket of water. The rest of the sodality meeting proved anticlimactic.

Because of my height (I like to think) I was always cast as a male in the plays at Our Lady of Angels. In my senior year, when we produced *Pharaoh's Daughter* for

the delectation of our parents and friends, I was cast as
Rameses Moesis, son of Pharaoh's daughter, who emerged
as Moses and led the people out of Egypt. This, was, of
course, a meaty role, more suited to Charlton Heston than
to me, and it was made even more impressive by the fact
that the entire play was rendered in blank verse. Sister
M. St. Matthew did the directing. Sometimes I awake at
night with a chill; I am back on the stage at OLA and
have forgotten the lines of *Pharaoh's Daughter!* Twenty-
four years have passed, and I suppose the phantom will
fade with time, but I still shake with fright at the fear
this nightmare engenders.

Actually, the production went off with comparatively
few mishaps. During one scene, striding onstage and discovering a slave driver beating an old Jew, I was supposed
to fell the lout with one well-aimed blow. He was to hit
his head on a stone pillar and die. The actual scene went
a bit awry. I swung as masculine a fist as I could produce
and missed him completely, but he fell on schedule. When
the other slave driver announced that he was dead, I
heard a loud, low whistle from the rear of the auditorium
where Maudie's uncle was sitting. I felt myself die a little.
Maudie's uncle Al was the one person on earth I wanted
to impress favorably.

The sisters felt that an essential part of every girl's education was training in ballroom conduct. For this purpose
we had dances in the gym. A little orchestra was brought
in for these occasions. The room was decorated with
crepe paper and flowers, and a lovely silver service
gleamed from the buffet table. We all wore evening
gowns. Of course, there were no boys there. Just girls.

By senior year, however, when the faculty decided to
go along with the new trend of boy and girl friendships,

we had a dance out at Eagle Point Lodge to which we could import friends from our home towns. We felt at ease in our formal attire and there was none of the ghastly awkwardness which might have been expected.

The dance at Eagle Point was a first for OLA. It represented a kind of giant step for the dear sisters; what behind-the-scenes trepidation and misgiving they must have experienced, one can only guess. Anyway, I invited Maudie's uncle Al to come to the dance, and he did. He filled out my program sideways down every page. It was an exhilarating and wonderful evening. The lodge had been decorated, and there was a fire burning in the hearth. The sisters sat along the sidelines and regarded their young ladies with what seemed to us pleased satisfaction, and the orchestra seemed more at ease at the lodge than out at the school gym. We felt that we had truly grown up at last. We were calmly ready to take on the world, communism, and all.

About four years later, Maudie's uncle and I took on the world together.

St. Ignatius High School

In 1870, Father Damen gathered a little group of Jesuits about him in Chicago, and did the thing Jesuits do best: he founded a school and named it St. Ignatius College. It was the first institution of higher learning in Chicago. In the course of time it has spiraled into the cornucopia which has enriched the city with Loyola University, with its School of Law and College of Commerce, Stritch School of Medicine, and Loyola Prep School. The original St. Ignatius is now a college preparatory. Thousands of Chicago boys have entered at one end of these institutions, to emerge at the other end trained, alert, capable citizens of the city; men who enter the clergy, professions, or business world with the mental treasury of a Jesuit education. Tens of thousands of them have gone forth from the by-products of this original foundation, their minds formed in the liberal arts tradition of the humanities, regardless of the direction of their future vocation. Theirs have been souls strengthened and tempered in the caldron of Jesuit discipline; among them have been the most powerful influences upon my own life: my father; the Reverend Daniel A. Lord, S.J.; the doctor who brought my children into the world, and the doctor into whose care I entrusted their health; and many of our closest friends.

The original St. Ignatius still stands today, its noble façade marked by nearly one hundred years of slow accumulation of the grit of a decaying neighborhood. Within its walls, and on its ancient stairs, crowd the newest

contingent of youth; within its walls, St. Ignatius is age-
less. The student body is hardly aware of the tradition
that is theirs; but before leaving St. Ignatius for the last
time, each of them will have been touched individually
and formed into something Ignatian.

Today only a few of these students actually live near
the school. The vast majority of them arise around six in
the morning and traverse a lengthy route before arriving
in time for the first class. Over 60 per cent of the boys
travel to Twelfth Street from the far South Side. Another
large group come from the West Side and the western
suburbs. But no distance seems too great, nor too difficult
to manage. Over two hundred parishes are represented
at St. Ignatius at the present time.

My father loved St. Ignatius with a depth that bordered
on idolatry. He had only to know that a stranger had gone
there; the stranger dissolved into a friend. The highest
accolade he could bestow upon a man was to say, with
just a touch of pride,

"Of course he's outstanding—he went to St. Ignatius,
you know." Years later, when at sixteen I became acquainted with that great apostle of youth, Father Lord,
Dad's first estimate of his fabled ability was based on the
fact that Father, too, had graduated from his old school.

The school in the early days was set in the middle of a
prairie. There is the usual talk about old-timers having
been able to see Lake Michigan from its tower. The city
surrounded it, flourished about its feet, began to wane,
and finally picked up her skirts and moved south, west,
and northward, while St. Ignatius stayed on. Finally, it
was the only little pocket of culture within miles.

Isolated in the vacuum left in the wake of the shifting
tide of the city, St. Ignatius went calmly on its academic

way. The halls ringing with Greek and Latin, the science department maintaining pace with the latest discoveries, so that when a group of Russian scientists inspected the Chicago high schools recently, they announced that the laboratory equipment of St. Ignatius was the finest they had seen.

Jug, that hallowed kingdom of the afterthought, has changed only slightly over the years. In my father's day, jug meant memorizing many lines of Greek poetry. My brother Tom jugged at Loyola twenty-five years later, was given English poetry to memorize; he still knows the whole of *Thanatopsis* and *Evangeline*, as a result of his frequent sojourning in jug. Today, unfortunates in jug are given either written compositions or, as a result of the high cost of school maintenance, janitorial service.

Parents all over the city have wistfully inquired why St. Ignatius wasn't moved farther west, or south. Loyola was north, and their beautiful new academy adequately answers the need in that section of Chicago. But the powers that be were loathe to move the old school, and the boys continue to hitchhike to St. Ignatius from all points of the compass.

Recently, the publication of the University of Illinois' proposed plan for a campus adjoining St. Ignatius has brought a new hope into being. By 1969, the entire neighborhood around St. Ignatius will be one vast campus, housing the thousands of students from the Navy Pier branch of the University of Illinois. With this renewal in mind, the Jesuits have decided to rebuild St. Ignatius for the coming century of scholars—right there on the same ground where it has always stood.

The old school building will be preserved as a priests' residence until it can be replaced. Rising up on the adjacent six-acre plot will be the new St. Ignatius, splendid and strong and modern. But when the old building is finally torn down, I hope some kindly minister in charge at the time will allow me to have one of those wolf's-head carvings which decorate the enormous main doors. I would cherish a memento of Chicago's first great school; remembering that this wooden sculpture felt the pressure of my father's hands, hands which formed so much of my happiness.

Father Lord, Apostle of Youth

The love of God and the love of neighbor, twin corner-
stones of the Judaeo-Christian ethic, are introduced to the
child shortly after solid foods, and are reiterated from
time to time in varying degrees of frequency and emphasis. It must have been the third grade sister who
taught me that the first three Commandments deal with
the love of God, and our duties stemming from that love;
while the remaining seven involve our neighbor, and our
obligation in regard to him. Intellectually, these exhorta-
tions have always been a part of my little mental store-
room, but it wasn't until I was a teenager that the
distinction between the letter and the spirit of the law became apparent to me, as well as the degree to which I had
devoted myself to the former to the detriment of the latter.

It was a priest who made this clear to me; not by words,
for his words were of gay, chatty things like books, plays,
interesting people he had met, or an amusing incident—
a million kaleidoscopic bits and pieces, but never a sermon. It was the man himself, the valorous, grace-touched
mind and heart of him, that showed me the difference.

Father Daniel A. Lord, S.J., was National Director of
the Sodality of Our Lady when I met him at the Summer
School of Catholic Action at the Morrison Hotel in Chicago, in 1936. He was fifty-one years old, with iron-gray
hair and eyes of incredible blue that looked deep into the
heart and found good in everyone. Present at the convention were about fifteen hundred young people from all

over the Middle West. The Summer School staff at that time consisted of a number of Jesuits and laymen, among them Fathers Gerald Ellard, Herbert Walker, and Roger Lyons. For a solid week these men guided us through a program of learning that touched upon literature, liturgy, effective speaking, the encyclicals, ideals of social justice, and the formation of a spiritual life. Evenings at the SSCA were given over to dances, amateur shows, skits, and songfests.

Moving through this complex as its motivator, impresario, director, announcer, and pivot was Father Lord, a whirlwind of energy. He literally lifted all of us beyond the barriers of strangled shyness at the beginning of the week into a cohesive group of Catholic young people. By the end of the week it seemed to us that prayers at the finish of an evening's dancing were the most natural and likely manner in which to end it.

Father Lord loved all men. He loved them as Christ loved them, with a completely disinterested regard for their color, age, or condition of life. He had an amazing faculty for seeing in the least prepossessing a quality that he could appreciate and enjoy. Music was, for him, the most natural means of communication between people. Father found that, loosened and relaxed by a few harmonious chords, the most dissimilar could somehow find common ground. He played the piano with an abandon and joy that has seldom been duplicated. He sang in a voice that was a kind of joyous speech rather than truly song. Lyrics were what he wished to convey. He counted on the piano to convey the tune.

Father became a close friend of the family, simply because he was instantly the friend of everyone who approached him with an outstretched hand. He had the

entire clan trained in Gilbert and Sullivan so that as he
walked into our house, he would shout in his booming
voice:

"My noble crew, good morning," to which we would
dutifully sing:

"Sir, good morning," upon which he would dash to the
piano, fling it open, and complete the entire song from
Pinafore, using us as a chorus.

When I was married, he simply transferred to the piano
at our apartment, and the room would ring with song
during his entire visit. My husband and I often took him
to restaurants for dinner, since my own cooking was still
shaky. He would immediately begin to question the waitress about how she liked her job: whereupon he would be
served snatches of her life story along with the meal, and
more often than not she would obtain Father's address so
she could write him about some problem. Father never
confined his ministry to a particular area. Anyone he met,
anywhere he happened to be, he was a priest ordained
for the people's sake, in order to help them to God.

It was natural that Father Lord's opinion on a wide
variety of subjects became mine. No one is so completely
imitative as an impressionable teenager. He spent con-
siderable time relaying to me his thoughts on everything
from beauty to the latest Broadway musical. One of his
noteworthy observations on feminine grooming was, "The
girl earning fifteen dollars a week (which dates the statement), who spends it on a permanent wave, is doing her
part to make the world a lovelier place in which to live."
He abhorred the fixed look of the professional model with
her posturings and affectation; he gave his wholehearted
approval to a beauty that was neat, well-groomed, and
clean. His mother's dictum that a lady was never without

a suggestion of good perfume was passed on to the gan-
gling adolescents he led like a Pied Piper into young adult-
hood. I've wondered from time to time what he would
have thought of the eagle's nests and raccoon eyes affected
by young girls today.

His advice on child rearing was invaluable, and remarkably useful. We have had many occasions to be grateful
for his wisdom and shrewd appraisal of the parent-child
relationship. The very young child was largely theory to
Father Lord, however. I recall one of his first visits after
Ann's birth. He swooped down on her with his usual vigor
and thundering cries of cheery reunion, put his smiling
face into her crib, and bellowed:

"Hi ya, small fry," whereupon Ann began to scream
with fright, much to his dismay. We had to spend some
time reassuring him that she was normal. He finally sheep-
ishly admitted that children usually reacted to him in this
incomprehensible fashion until they reached the age of
four or five; and it was so. Yet, as our children reached
the age of reason, they became his slaves. Before that
time, they viewed him from a distance.

Father Lord loved a picnic. Whenever a speaking en-
gagement or retreat brought him close enough for an
afternoon of relaxation, he would write and warn us that
a picnic was due. This occasioned preparations on the
grand scale, for he usually wrote about twenty other
friends and alerted them that we were all going together;
his formula for picnics being quite simple: the more the
merrier. We would find a caravan of cars lined up at the
appointed hour, and Father, in old white trousers, joyfully directing them all out to the Dunes, or the Forest
Preserves, or wherever his fancy had decided would be
the ideal spot. There we would meet (those of us who

hadn't gotten lost on the way) and he would direct the cooking, table setting, games, singing, and whatever other activity he could conjure up. Sometimes he would bring along a book he wanted to read to us. It might be Irish ghost stories, or poems, or something new he thought we might like.

Father Lord possessed a vigor that was almost super-human. His notion of relaxing was to fling himself at a piano and play for four hours without a break. The musi-cal shows he produced and directed in St. Louis, Detroit, and Canada were gigantic undertakings involving thou-sands; they were delightful little diversions to Father. I often watched him backstage at these spectacles, which resembled De Mille sets in scope. He would mill about happily, in an old sweatshirt, listening to worried young men with lists, joking with Negro high school kids who had fast rhythm numbers in all his shows, and praising with sincere warmth the group that had just finished re-hearsing.

His technique was basic. He knew the ache of the young to be noticed and approved. He drilled them until they were worthy of praise, and then he poured it over their grateful heads like oil. Father detested flattery. He could grow fiercely angry at insincerity or the fables of press agents. When he spoke to young people he spoke with love, appreciation, wit, and joyfulness, and we felt ourselves grow tall under the warm sun of his approval. We wanted desperately to earn that praise, and we strove beyond our puny selves to win it.

Hoards of young men and women followed in the spar-kling wake of this dynamic Jesuit. A lesser man might have become proud, and attempted to capitalize on this adulation. Father Lord gently turned the current of our love to the Source of his life and work. He was content to be God's middleman.

The last ten years of Father's life were years of painful suffering. He had cancer of the lung, but he kept on working until two months before he died. I flew to St. Louis, and it was at the funeral of this beloved friend that I realized fully the meaning of the love which overflowed from his great heart into the lives of everyone he met. For I found hundreds of people whose lives had been similarly transformed by him.

Father Lord was buried with all the honors the city of St. Louis could give him. An archbishop said a Pontifical Funeral Mass. A bishop gave the sermon. The mayor of St. Louis, every prominent Catholic for miles around, judges, doctors, professors, great men from every field came to bid him good-by.

But the congregation which overflowed that college church preached the finest sermon of all. For as I looked about through tear-filled eyes, I saw the people he had loved, his neighbors. Some were laboring men in heavy shoes, their wives in colored babushkas. Some were Negro men and women weeping unashamedly. There were young nurses in uniform, dark-skinned foreign students, tired old Irishmen, prosperous merchants, Chinese, society women; people, in short, from every walk of life, from every condition and age of life. All had loved this man, and had been loved by him.

The funeral wound its way through the bitterly cold January snow to Florissant, and the little Jesuit cemetery where he was laid to rest. When we entered the grounds of Florissant, his fellow Jesuits met us in procession, singing the Office for the Dead. The wind carried their mournful chant to us, and turned our tears to ice. But his care for us was still evident, for there was a huge canopy over the ground where the grave had been prepared; one that sheltered us all, and cut back the wind. Like his love, it hung over all our heads, and we huddled together there, about three hundred of us, rich, poor, young, old, clerics, and lay people. We looked into one another's eyes that morning and saw no distinctions; only a common grief for the lost friend whose great soul had engulfed us all.

Where Dainty Phlox, etc.

"A Garden is a lovesome thing, God wot!" sang the poet of old; and if our little back yard can be dignified by the name of garden, and if the poet's "lovesome" means lovable, then he certainly hit the nail on the head! For our garden is the most lovable place in our domain; a well-used, bug-ridden, haphazard, lovesome yard, God wot!

When we were house hunting we developed a system, Al and I, for proper appraisal of a given property. I counted the closets and the number of blocks to the Catholic school, and Al measured the amount of lawn he would have to mow. It was discouraging at times, for the big roomy houses with dozens of closets invariably had the kind of lawn Al described as a golf course—one which would be growing in the far corners as fast as he could mow the rest of it. What he wanted, he claimed, was a concrete yard. Painted green, perhaps. He once toyed with the idea of inventing a lawn made of shaved green rubber which would have all the springiness of grass and none of its annoying propensity to growth.

Fourteen years ago, when we finally found the house, it had nine closets, was one block from school, and had a tiny handkerchief of lawn, flanked by a concrete driveway and patio combined. Al took one look at the lawn and bought the house immediately.

The following spring, in May, we were awarded the nicest bonus ever bestowed upon mortgaged mortals. We awoke one morning to find that those giant bushes near the back picket fence were lilacs, delicate and fragrant; Persian and French in white and two shades of lavender, filling the tiny yard with beauty, and us with unbelieving wonder. For days we walked around them, picking armloads for vases, grandly bestowing them on lilacless neighbors and reveling in their loveliness. We bought a lawn chair so we could sit and look at them. Their wholly unexpected and delightful presence was the beginning of gardening in our tiny yard.

The bushes are twenty-five feet high and grow in a semicircle, with the lawn timidly edging up to a shade line, but not beyond. The shaded area is about ten feet deep, and I decided to try to find a plant that would grow there. Many trials later, we found the best plant to be impatiens, in pink shades; and we dug some fern from the yard at Mother and Dad's and planted this at the back edges near the picket fence.

Now the little yard had color after the lilacs faded, and we began to dream of having a statue there in the lilac shade. It would have to be a Mary shrine—of an outdoor material, and large enough to be in scale with the giant bushes. Thus began the search for a Queen for the garden.

Abandoning the statuary houses as too expensive after we were offered an outdoor statue one and one-half feet high for one hundred and fifty dollars, I began driving through the countryside in search of old statues which might have been abandoned in favor of the newer and less beautiful polished stones in the cemeteries. I came across many old statues in this search; most of them sorrowing angels holding wreaths. One of these was solemnly offered to me as a statue of the Blessed Mother.

"But those wings," I said to the eager salesman, "that's an angel."

"Nah," he insisted, "they just added those to make it look good. That's her all right."

I looked once more at the Angel of Death with the wreath held aloft and one foot already poised for flight, and said it wouldn't do.

And then I found her. I was driving down a back road near a monument company and caught a glimpse of her crowned head and the Babe's sweet face. The statue was overgrown with weeds and was very old. I almost ran to the man leaning against the shed.

"How much do you want for the Virgin and Child?"

He looked at me and smilingly shook his head.

"You don't want that, lady—it's broken." We went over and drew aside the tall weeds. It was Our Lady of Mount Carmel, holding the Child in her arms; a bit marred from time. Fingers were missing from her outstretched hand and the infant's foot was gone. It was pitted, weather-scarred Italian marble, but of excellent workmanship, and the age only added to its beauty. She stood four feet high; perfect for the lilac shrine, and I told the man why I wanted her. He turned out to be a prince in overalls. He gave her to me, along with a granite stone to stand her on, with instructions about the ready-mix cement with which to affix the statue to the stone and then had his men load both into the rear of the station wagon. I drove off, with the car at a crazy angle, singing prayers of gratitude.

But as I backed the car down the driveway at home I began to wonder how in the world I would ever unload four hundred pounds of marble and granite. I opened the car door and sat there. It was thirty feet from the drive to the lilac bushes and it had taken three men to load the stone into the car.

"First things first," I thought, and drove out the driveway again to the hardware store for the ready-mix cement. And as I backed into the parking place in front of the store, who should be coming out but three large men in overalls—street construction workers on their lunch hour!

Fifteen minutes later Our Lady stood cemented to her granite stone under her lilac shrine. Total cost for the three musketeers: six dollars. They left, and I knelt down to beg her to bless our yard, be the protectress of our home, the guardian of our children, and the Queen of our hearts. In all the years she has stood there, no child has ever been hurt in our yard, though they climb to the garage roof and up into the trees. I know she is watching over us still.

In winter, she and her Son gaze steadily out from under snow-laden boughs and watch the snow fights and sledding. But for the three other seasons we determined that she would have beautiful flowers around her, and that is when gardening swung into high gear.

Roses, we decided; ever blooming roses, the best we could afford. And for years now, every birthday, Mother's Day and Easter, Al and the children give me, not cut flowers, but rose bushes for the yard. We couldn't plant them in front of the statue, because of the shade. So we cut a large circle in the handkerchief lawn and planted five rose bushes there. Two Peace, two Chrysler Imperial, and one Twilight. At the very center, we planted Regale lily bulbs. The first year they bloomed, alternating with red and pink roses, they created a sight that was unforgettable. All spring, summer, and fall, the roses bloomed and we picked the last one the day before Thanksgiving.

Al, the garden hater, could be found every morning after breakfast in the middle of the yard, calling us to come out and see the rose that was just opening. More roses were added each year. When no more would fit in the yard, we marched them down the edge of the driveway.

Today, bulb plantings give spring a gay greeting: jonquils, hyacinths, and tulips to herald the lilac. Deep in the lilac shade, violets hide near the statue and await the roses. Midsummer, the pure Regale lilies raise their lovely heads from the rose circle and nod to the Queen and Her Son. Delicate phlox, carnations and daisies, petunias, iris, ageratum, marigolds, impatiens, day lilies and scabiosa hold forth until the mums begin, and these are still burning brightly as the autumn skies darken and the first snow falls. It's truly surprising, the variety of bloom possible in a small yard.

The concrete drive and patio area are continually busy too. The snow forts give way to jump ropes and roller skates, and the bounding basketball perils the freshly budding plants. Yard lights prolong the usefulness of our yard, and the purchase of a barbecue unfolded another area for exploration. Shish kebab we discovered, and charcoal broiled Italian sausages; chicken slowly turning on the spit; steaks, hamburgers, wieners, and even crisp liver and bacon have made outdoor meals a family institution.

At the present time we are trying to think of a way to shade the table that will be effective and economical. For all through the nice weather we have lunch and dinner outdoors. Occasionally, we breakfast there too.

When I was a child, my mother used to sing a song that went:

> That bird with feathers of blue
> Is waiting for you,

Back in your own back yard;
You'll find your happiness lies
Right under your eyes,
Back in your own back yard.

I'm teaching it to my children now. In a world that daily grows more troubled, I want them always to remember the little yard where the Queen reigned, and where life was sweet and unclouded. We want them to go out from there and find yards of their own to tend, and flowers of their own to grow. We think it's an important part of living.

Chez Anton

Remember Groucho Marx's blasé rejoinder (in a movie the title of which I've forgotten) when someone complimented him upon his palatial mansion: "It's forty-seven rooms and a swimming pool, but the FHA and I call it home." Ours has seven and a half rooms, but the mortgage company and seven of us call it home.

Home is where the heart is. Home is what it takes a heap o'livin' to make a house into. But you get the idea! We love ours.

Al and I think that homes are for living, loving, and entertaining in. We are not of the cocktail set. I am not the remarkable culinary queen who can turn out petit fours, or hors d'oeuvre from leftover salmon, peanut butter, and anchovy paste. We offer highballs to those who want them, and are always out of ginger ale. Our children have perfected terrier instincts that can root out the hiding places as quickly as we can stash away soft drinks. But our friends come anyway.

We give little dinners, but not often. Our table every evening is graced with seven people, and this involves a preparation and execution which keeps me so busy I seldom dream of attempting formal little dinners that look so well in the woman's pages. There is often an extra place at table, but our motto is: let's get this clambake over with so we can settle down with the guests who will be here later for coffee.

It's a lead-pipe cinch that someone will be here for coffee.

The coffee crew is varied and select. There is a Dominican who plays bongo drums and accompanies his pleasant voice on a ukelele. There is a couple who are professional artists and fill our evenings with music. There is a Jesuit of properly scholastic appearance who harbors an insane passion for stew, and loves fixing things that go awry at Chez Anton. In the past three years he has fixed the handles on all the pots and pans, made an address sign and affixed it to a tree in front of the house, constructed numerous little shelves, and wired several lamps. He has a way with Billy, our youngest, and is forever bringing him little gifts.

"Hi ya, stupid," he greets Bill. And Bill comes racing to his arms ready for the swing high in the air.

There are friends of long standing, and brand new ones we've just met. All of them are dear to us. They add the indispensible ingredient every home needs—the opportunity to exercise hospitality.

The war years brought many changes in the average household; ours was no exception. Walls were strained to make room for the homeless, as empty apartments became scarce as hen's teeth. Barriers came tumbling down and strangers were taken into our homes in a general spirit of co-operation. One heard of the valiant spirit of the English enduring nightly air raids, and it seemed shameful not to do a little extra when we were lucky enough to be out of firing range.

There were three children in the seven-room house then. By rearrangement of bedrooms, we could free one room upstairs which was given to a young married couple who had been evicted from their apartment by the landlord to make room for his returning GI son. The recreation

room in the basement became the nest of two Irishmen
my brother had met in Ireland, and casually invited to
visit. They did, and so entranced us that they stayed three
years.

Home during these years took on the flavor and color
of Grand Hotel. Every evening was filled with discussion,
song, games, and laughter. Every morning was rigidly
scheduled into twenty-minute units for the bathroom and
kitchen. The children stayed in bed until the adults had
departed for their respective offices.

Joe and Seamus were about the same age, twenty-three,
and it was difficult to understand how two such different
characters could maintain so close and strong a bond of
friendship. They had grown up in the same little town in
Northern Ireland, and gone all through school together.
Joe was terse, practical, highly intelligent, keen-eyed and
thrifty. Seamus was charming, spendthrift, poetic, dreamy,
and forever getting lost. He once called the house in des-
peration and fearfully said into the phone:

"Joe—this is Seamus here. Where am I?" Joe efficiently
ascertained (by means of a street guide he always carried
in his pocket) Seamus' exact position. He carefully out-
lined the steps Seamus was to take; which bus, where to
transfer, how far to walk, all with the patient manner one
would use with an idiot. One hour later, Seamus called
again, this time practically in tears. He had of course
taken the right bus, but it went the wrong way, and he
was now on the far South Side. Wearily Joe directed the
stray lamb until he finally arrived home hours later, safe,
hungry, and pathetically grateful for having been found
at last.

As they were nearly the same size, Joe always bought

their clothes with a view to joint use, and he purchased them in the better bargain basements. This frugality wounded the sensitive soul of Seamus. One day on the porch, he complained bitterly about the cheap shoes Joe had bought, alleging they had given him blisters. Al kindly asked why he didn't remove the shoes.

"I can't," said Seamus with dignity, "because Joe has a hole in these socks!"

They had an unfailing humor and a wild enthusiasm for things American, which is typical of every Irishman I ever met. Joe told us that as a boy he remembers his mother taking him atop Cave Hill near Belfast and pointing out the direction of Rome and of America. He never forgot those directions. He is now an American citizen and a Catholic priest.

Seamus loved to go shopping in the big Loop stores with me, much to my husband's consternation. Seamus was always egging me on to buy things. I remember a day at Field's art gallery, when I saw a lovely painting of a farm scene, and Seamus talked me into buying it for Al's birthday (five months away). I protested that I didn't have enough money.

"Put it on the Kathleen Mavourneen,"* said Seamus firmly.

"What in the world is that?" I inquired.

"You know, it may be for years, and it may be forever!" sang Seamus. We bought the painting.

The death of one of our friend's parents was the occasion for Seamus to attend his first American wake. He was scandalized, and could hardly wait to see Joe.

"Joe," he said with great excitement, "whatever you're

* A popular Irish expression for a time-payment plan.—Ed.

planning for tomorrow night, drop it. This wake is something you've got to see. They put lipstick and rouge on
the poor man, Joe, and he's done up like a dressmaker's
dummy. You must see it, Joe. It's in a big place, like a
hotel lobby, and everyone stands around and talks. I half
expected to be served a wee cocktail any minute."

We asked them about the wakes we'd heard about in
Ireland. They were both quite firm about it.

"When a person dies in Ireland," said Seamus, "he is
laid out in a shroud in his own living room, with a cross
on his chest. No one puts pancake make-up on him; they
all know he's dead, so they don't mind if he looks dead.
And they all take off work next day to go round to the
Mass and the burial." We said no more about that. Apparently the song "The Night Pat Murphy Died," one of
Father Cahill's favorites, was largely myth.

One of Joe's aunts, Auntie Finn, had wheeled a baby
buggy filled with rifles under the noses of the British
during the "troubles." Seamus' father had been an officer
in the British Army. Both boys had seen service in World
War II, Seamus in Iceland, and Joe in London. They were
mild-mannered, gentle-voiced, and courteous. The family
finally forgot they were not blood relatives and the children introduced them as "my big brothers."

The boys were wonderful with the children. On their
days off they walked all over Chicago and Oak Park.
Walking was their creed, their exercise, and their pleasure.
When they first arrived, they walked daily to the post
office to send cards home, being unaware of the function
of the mail box.

"Sure, it's only a short hop," they'd say, and take off for
a point five miles' distant.

Contemplating the American child was a continual

source of delight and amazement to them. Child rearing in Ireland, I gathered, was handled a bit differently. They never quite got used to the constant attention, numerous toys, overprotectiveness, and piano, skating, or dancing lessons with which the American tot was encumbered. They watched Al and me trying to be good parents, and while we felt they applauded our efforts, we were also aware that they pondered about the emphasis on "social integration with the group" instead of a firmer discipline. Theirs had been a stern school. Instead of psychology, a swift hand to the seat of the trouble was employed. Children in Ireland were seen more than heard, and indeed, seldom seen. For this reason, I think, the conversation of our children was an unending source of comment and speculation.

Joe spent his free Saturday afternoons taking Sarge, aged five, and Laurie, who was three, to the movies. Arriving home, he would report Sarge's exact comments while viewing the picture, after making certain the children were beyond earshot. He has an amazing memory, and a filing-cabinet mind, so that he can relate about one hundred of these conversations with the children even after all these years. This, of course, assures him a ready audience, since there is nothing children love more than to hear the "cute" things they got off so effortlessly as babies.

Seamus and Joe argued endlessly about events they interpreted from their opposite temperaments. Quiet summer evenings were frequently punctuated with such sentiments as:

"Ach, Seamus, you're daft! It wasn't that way at all!" To which Seamus would answer:

"I'm not so, knucklehead, it's just that I've a far greater capacity for understanding and insight!"

But they remained steadfast friends just the same.

Seamus told us about the parade in Dublin during a feast day celebration. All the shopkeepers had co-operated along the line of march whence the procession would come by decorating their store fronts with banners and appropriate signs. Seamus swears that one of these read, "God bless the Sacred Heart!" I love to think that this is true.

We found Irishisms slipping into our conversation.

"Smart? She's so smart she could talk to the rent man!" Or, when a celebration was clearly called for:

"Let's do it up right—give the cat the canary."

Some of these caused the boys trouble. Seamus was handed a photograph of the wife of one of his fellow workers at the steel company.

"My," said Seamus with great enthusiasm, "isn't she a fine, homely girl!" He found out moments later that "homely" is not the same in America as it is in Ireland.

Seamus developed a great fondness for lemon juice and water, which he called energy juice. He was always heading for the glider on the front porch with a glass of energy juice, for the announced purpose of "resting his little frame." There he would hold forth for an hour or more with anyone who had the leisure to listen about a perfectly fascinating book he had just come across, or a bit of philosophy he was trying on for size. Somewhere in his past had been a prolonged exposure to *Hansel and Gretel*, the Humperdinck operetta. He sang this through from beginning to end, taking all the parts himself, and amusing the children for hours. He also told them seemingly incredible stories about the Irish giant, Finn Mac-

Cool. Joe would stand this for as long as possible, and then counter with the "Once more unto the breach" speech from *Henry V*, which he did with phrasing that would have curled Olivier's hair with envy. Between the two of them, we had no need for TV. They were infinitely more entertaining than the best show on television.

The boys took care of their own laundry and cleaning. Joe spent hours darning his socks with a little mechanical device he had bought in Canada—a kind of miniature loom. His mother always sent along an extra ball of yarn she knit his socks from, and this was carefully threaded onto the little loom and cleverly woven into a perfect darn. He took great pride in those hand-knit socks. He wore them in ninety-five-degree weather, and claimed that they were actually cooler than the cotton socks men wore in America. Apparently they were right for Joe, anyway, because he walked endlessly every day without tiring.

When Joe finished his seminary training and was ordained Father Malachy, we had the first Mass at our parish church, and our friends and family joined us in the celebration. Sarge was an altar boy at the great event, vested with the job of Master of Ceremonies. Aside from a great deal of backfield huddling with the subdeacon, which I could not recall as being part of the rubrics, I thought Sarge served the Mass very well. Malachy even sang the Preface on key. The family knelt in the front pew and flooded the place with happy tears. Receiving Holy Communion for the first time from our Joe was one of the happiest moments of our lives. His priesthood added a new dimension in happiness to all our days, and his visits home are filled with music, wonderful anecdotes, and laughter.

Seamus went on to New York, where he is following a successful career in a publishing house, and furnishing his bachelor quarters on the Kathleen Mavourneen plan. Malachy is stationed in New Jersey at the present time, and sometimes has occasion to visit Seamus. Seamus reports that Malachy goes through his clothing, picking out things to take back to the seminary with him. "I never buy anything black anymore," says Seamus, "because Malachy would take it back to his boys before I had a chance to wear it!"

The Father of Chez Anton

One of the best ways a man can learn to be a wise and
patient father is to manage to be born into a family pre-
sided over by a wise and patient father, whom he then
can imitate. Older sons in particular can benefit from this
strategy, for they can watch their father coping with the
younger children, and observe how he strives to do what
is best for them, without succumbing to the more obvious
pitfalls of overindulgence or severity. My husband, who
was the youngest son of a family whose father had died
young, had no such opportunity to observe and learn. His
only contact with children younger than himself was with
the barely noticed young fry of his neighborhood, who
entered his consciousness rarely, if at all. It is to his
eternal credit that he came to fatherhood with practically
no aptitudes at hand, and has evolved into a truly talented
father.

His being Polish by descent, I am convinced, was a
tremendous asset. Poles are traditionally good parents;
vitally concerned with their family life, willing to sacri-
fice for the good of the family, and passionately desirous
for the happiness of their children. But, besides being
of Polish descent, Al had no other help than his keen
sense of humor. Between these two assets, he built and
developed a fatherhood that is the clear result of the
nuptial graces.

His early days as a father were heroic. Small Ann,
whom he loved with a devotion that kept him hovering

near her crib if she as much as whimpered, was too tiny for him to hold comfortably. He tried it, gingerly, and finally gave up. He claimed that every muscle in his arms and back ached from the strain of holding her without crumpling, dropping, or injuring her. Beads of perspiration stood out on his brow every time I placed her in his arms. Finally he asked if he could defer holding her until she "tightened up a bit." He sat by her crib and sang to her instead. When any of the children were sick, his agony until they were well again was harder to cope with than the illness itself. The sight of the doctor calmly probing a sore throat filled him with such anger he would have to leave the room until the ordeal was over.

Marriage brings out all sorts of unsuspected talents and aptitudes. Many a man who couldn't tell one end of a hammer from the other gets married and winds up paneling the basement. Al surprised me by turning out to be a terrific cook. Sunday breakfast soon became his special feast, and our favorite meal. Sarge claims that coming out of St. Giles Church (two blocks away) he can smell the bacon and sausages Daddy is preparing in the kitchen. Al's scrambled eggs are light and creamy and he lovingly works them around in the pan with the chopped bits of bacon he has previously prepared, while the coffee perks and the toast is browning. His fame is so widespread that we seldom get beyond the orange juice before casual callers begin arriving for coffee. This is where Al truly shines. He loves nothing more than being host to our friends and hearing them rave about his cooking.

Saturday is his soup day, during the nippy months. He has a huge pot simmering on the back of the stove all day long, and keeps tending it with dashes of condiments and inspired additions from the pantry, between halves of the football game or commercials during the golf matches on TV.

Businesswise, as we say on Madison Avenue, Al is a steel trap. A food broker, he can quote prices and percentages from three months back, and knows everything about his customer's business statistics. He knows who in Chicago uses a special cut of coconut, and why. What he can't remember is to mail a letter I give him in the morning. They say the mind can hold just so much information before the files jam, and I guess this is what has happened. Al's mental file is so chuck full of business data that he must rely on outside help for such minor recollections as when to get a hair cut and what it was I wanted at the drug store. Through the years he has developed a defense mechanism so acute that whenever he is called from a distance he answers, "Did I what?" instead of, "What do you want?" Sample: the phone rings for Al while he is in the bathtub. I shout upstairs to deliver the message.

"Al, your brother wants to know if you're playing poker with them tonight!" From the bathroom echoes his stock phrase: "Did I what?"

Or, in the middle of the night when I wake up shivering and gently shake him to unwind the blankets.

"Did I what?" says Al in his sleep.

Al's mother, a dear little Polish lady, had a pessimism that extended to every phase of living. Her love for her sons was great, and we finally learned to hide from her the fact that they sometimes traveled by plane. She would have them dead and buried in her mind before they reached their fishing grounds. The slightest suggestion of illness sounded fatal to Mom, and she worried over colds and headaches as though they were symptoms of cancer.

"Just wait," she would say sadly, "bieda is coming." "Bieda" is Polish for hard times.

Mom's memory was excellent, though in her later years it developed an off again, on again quality, which caused many misunderstandings, and made for fascinating conversation. Al took her shopping every Saturday, and used to lunch with her afterward, chatting about the past or playing cards for a while after lunch. One day he said to her:

"Mom, do you remember the wedding present you gave to Rita and me?" Mom shook her head sadly and said she couldn't recall.

"Don't you remember, Mom? It was a coffee can filled with quarters." Mom looked across the table at him with real interest.

"Did I do that?" she said.

"You sure did," said Al. "There was seventy-five dollars in that can!"

"There was one hundred and seventeen dollars in the can," snapped Mom.

Al worries too, but his pessimism is softened and graced with a saving sense of humor that has allowed him to find, ultimately, the funny side of things. Some of his habits of worry go back into the hidden depths of heritage, and will never really be eased. Some are the kind he can be talked out of. But there are some worries that stem from defective drains, faulty roofing, and sagging porches. This kind of worry is compounded by the knowledge that as the condition worsens, the cost of repair work is spiraling. But the worst kind of worry Al suffers is brought on by heavy rains.

Some years ago we turned our basement into a recreation area. We paneled the walls, converted the furnace, removed pipes, and made it a combination library and study room. It has given us great pleasure, added room for living, and afforded new space for the children to entertain friends. But when it rains, Al cannot sleep at night. He is certain that the moment he shuts his eyes, a torrential flood will gush into the basement via the crack under the back door, and ruin the paneling. It is true that there have in the past five years been occasions when water has seeped in. It trickles down the grade to the laundry room, where it collects around the floor drain. There has never been the slightest damage, though it is a nuisance to wipe up. But Al is convinced that someday while his back is turned the basement will be flooded under two feet of water. This nightmare haunts his dreams, and has spoiled what used to be a real pleasure in rain. During heavy storms he refuses to go to bed. He keeps a lonely vigil by the basement door, waiting for the deluge.

Al grew up in St. Bartholomew's Parish, and was a member of the young people's club there. Every year saw a major dramatic production by this group, memorable in family archives as comedies, though not all of them were intended as such. Al's two brothers were also in the club, and from what I hear of *Seven Keys to Baldpate*, as rendered by the St. Bartholomew's players, there were some striking departures from the original script. It seems that the burden of summer rehearsals caused an oversight on the part of the prop department. They overlooked the fact that most of the action was to take place in winter, and it wasn't until the day the play was to be presented that they remembered about the heavy winter clothing this story required. The play is centered around a single room, into which a long succession of characters come, each doffing during his opening lines an overcoat, hat, scarf, gloves, overshoes, and so on. Al claims that by the time he hit the stage, midway in the first act, he was unable to find any furniture in evidence. Coats were draped all over the chairs, all the tables and bookcases had been completely covered with haberdashery, while overshoes littered the stage underfoot. He picked his way through the maelstrom, looking in vain for an empty chair on which to place his overcoat and finally selected the only floor lamp on the stage. He said his opening line, draped his coat over the lamp, and plunged the set into semidarkness. The audience went wild.

Al operates on the live and let live theory. We lived for a time in an old house which harbored mice, and I simply couldn't get the hang of baiting a mouse trap. I tried every known powder, poison, and strategy to rid the premises of these swift, silent, and unwelcome guests, but without success. Al came home one evening and announced that he had found the solution to the problem. A mouse, he stated, will always run along the baseboard of a room, right? Mice seldom cross an open space. Al, therefore, proposed to place a brown paper bag parallel to the baseboard, opened invitingly and perhaps even containing a little tidbit to eat. This he did, and then pretended to read the paper, waiting. Sure enough, before long a brown-streaked scurry told us the mouse was in the bag, and with one swift movement Al closed the opening and picked it up. From the angry scuffle inside, we judged that our mouse was unhappy in confinement.

The question of disposal was now uppermost. Al stood there for a moment, with a tiger by the tail, wondering what to do next. It was a bitterly cold January night. The snow was a foot deep outside, and Al decided, with characteristic pity, that the least painful death would be by freezing. He took the bagged mouse out to the yard, scooped out a little grave, and placed the bag in the snow. Then he raced back to the warmth of the house.

He fixed some coffee, and joined me in the living room. He finished reading his paper between sips and then tried solitaire. I was sewing, and noticed his growing restlessness. One hour passed, and then two. He made his nightly check on the furnace, began turning out lights in the living room, and was on the point of suggesting that we go up to bed when he said suddenly:

"That mouse must be frozen by now—I'll just run out and check on him." With that he opened the back door and skimmed out to the bag in the snow. Lifting it gently, he noticed no movement within. He thought for a moment about throwing bag and all into the garbage can in the alley, but at the last moment, opened the bag. A furry brown streak whizzed past him, up the back stairs and into the warm kitchen. I could hear his laughter all the way upstairs. He came in, still holding the bag.

Possibly the greatest heritage Al has been able to transfer to his children is his love of music. He sings in the choir every Sunday at a nearby church. His voice is a baritone with strong timbre and a pleasant quality. His brothers share this musical talent. Two of them, Vic and Will, used to sing with him in a trio. They are all still called upon at parties to entertain. Al does not play the piano, but he can sight-read any music, and was able to help the children at piano practice because his unerring ear could spot a false note or an uneven tempo instantly.

Some years ago, we decided to get a group of people together who shared this love of singing, and formed a singing club which makes up in volume what it lacks in

quality. We meet about twice a month, and are fortunate
to have as director and accompanist a two-piano team
known professionally as Gillette and Micari, who are
really Vera and Vincent Micari, two of our closest friends.
Vincent directs the singing group with a verve and zest
that keeps us striving for a better blend long after our
feet have numbed to the kneecaps. Vera plays the accompaniment with a perfection that often keeps us quiet just
listening to her pearly runs and magnificent mastery of
any music, great or small.

Al loves the singing club, and wouldn't dream of missing a session; but he loves it best when it is at our house
and he can be host. Then he commands the floor and
keeps everyone quiet so he can hear Vera play Chopin.

Al often says that selling is a joy—it's driving to the
accounts that kills him. Some of his trials with the car
have passed into legend. Like the time Al drove to the
Loop and parked the car for four or five hours in one of
those huge elevator parking lots. Upon completion of his
business, he went back to the lot to claim our blue station
wagon. He handed the ticket to the attendant, who went
away and came driving back in a yellow convertible. It
was a pretty car, but since it wasn't ours, Al refused to
take it. There was much huddling among the attendants,
who checked and rechecked his ticket and finally brought
the manager into the act. The manager dispatched about
five attendants to search the entire lot systematically for
the car.

An hour passed, and Al, by no means a placid individual, was seething and grinding his teeth and complaining
bitterly about the general inefficiency in evidence, when
the yellow convertible began to look vaguely familiar. The
remembrance suddenly struck him that his own car was

being repaired, and he had been driving his secretary's
yellow car for the day's business.

In the face of dilemma, Al chooses to be brief. He
simply stepped to the curb, quickly opened the convertible door and slid under the wheel. On the way out, he
whispered to the astounded Negro attendant:

"I just remembered—this *is* my car!" and left the
premises as fast as the speed laws would allow. His last
glance in the rear-view mirror clearly depicted the man's
open mouthed astonishment. To this day Al has never
gone back to that garage!

Father Cahill

We met Father Phil two weeks after our wedding. Having arranged our silver wedding presents in the dining room and stored away the creamy linens and untried appliances, we decided to make ourselves known at the parish house so that we would not be overlooked in the matter of weekly envelopes. We were innocent children in the big wide world.

My husband set the keynote for all our future relations with the clergy with his opening remark.

"My wife and I have carefully measured the distance between the Baptist church and home, and St. Sylvester's and home, and have decided to join up here."

Father Phil took the long black cigar out of his mouth, put his number eleven shoes up on the desk, and leaned back to ask:

"And just where is home?"

We told him where it was, invited him up to visit us, and from there on, he took over.

He baptized our first three children, was friend and adviser in the early years of our marriage, and proved one of the finest friends we were fortunate enough to find.

On him I tried my starkly original versions of rather staid recipes; he drank the first cup of what was laughingly called coffee. In the course of the next few months, he and Al moved our proud little collection of furniture into every conceivable position in the apartment, and back to first again. It got so he would come in, remove his collar, and say:

"OK—what do you want moved this evening?"

To a lesser man, this might have seemed an imposition. But Father Phil, in addition to the indelible mark on his soul, has one other attribute of which he is inordinately proud. He has muscles. These muscles have almost acquired an independent life of their own, for when he speaks of them it is with the quiet pride of one who modestly makes no extraordinary claim that the facts themselves cannot substantiate. Father's muscles have been sculpted with painstaking labor over a period of years. No device has gone untried—no training has been deemed too Spartan. In the tradition of the great Charles Atlas, Father Phil had once been a ninety pound weakling. The fact that he was eleven years old at the time has no bearing on the case. He determined that he would make of his body an instrument that would do his every bidding unquestioningly, and it is a tribute to his unconquerable will that he did just that. Though he is forty-nine years old today, he has never had a headache, or known a day's illness except for an excruciating period he spent with a slipped disc. And this magnificent health he freely attributes to a program of exercise strictly followed, and the grace of God.

An unwieldy piece of furniture is a challenge that brings a light to his eye. Once, upon passing a second-hand store and spying a huge roll-top desk in the window, he immediately went in and made it his own. He claims he needed it for his papers. I am of the firm opinion that he bought the monster just to see if he could carry it up the three flights of stairs of St. Malachy's rectory to his little room in the attic.

His method of attack was characteristic. When he maneuvered this gargantuan coffer into a trailer and carted it to the rectory, he found himself faced with the fact that even after removing the legs there was no possible way of ascending the staircase with a desk of these Leviathan proportions. So he opened his tool chest, selected a saw of the proper keenness, and calmly sawed it down the middle, and carried the pieces to his room, where he firmly bolted them together. He says the desk is a marvelous addition to his room, notwithstanding the fact that he can no longer close his closet door.

Along with his portable Mass kit, Father goes nowhere without his tools. He not only hauls carpenters' tools, mechanics' tools, plumbing tools, electric drills, and sanders; his car trunk also cradles a sledge hammer, several coils of rope, sink faucets, books, tire gauge, old jackets, a bucket of oats, miscellaneous rags and polishes, and what is undoubtedly the world's foremost collection of screw drivers. He needs these things with him at all times, he says, because he never knows what kind of situation he will run into in the course of a social evening with friends, a jaunt to his farm in Indiana, or the routine drive to Quigley Preparatory Seminary where he teaches Freshman English and Religion.

The funny thing about it is he's right. I would hate to count the times he has been called upon to fix the multifarious gadgets that are always suffering breakdowns at our house. And if one were to multiply these by the number of houses he visits, and then by the number of years he has been an ordained priest—he should really be given an honorary union card.

If Father Phil is ever canonized, I want first crack at painting him. I shall do a life-sized oil of a handsome

Irishman (muscular) with a shock of white hair rising above a pair of steady blue eyes. In one hand he will hold a chalice, and in the other, an electric drill. Behind him, drifting into an Indiana landscape, will be discerned several horses, a little farmhouse, a field of shamrocks, a row of books, a roll-top desk, a cement mixer, the hills of Ireland, and about a thousand friends.

If the Diocese of Chicago should ever go bankrupt, which seems highly unlikely, Father Cahill's talents as a used car dealer might go a long way toward restoring the use of black ink. No one is ever so disrespectful as actually to call him Madman Cahill, but there are striking resemblances between the famous Mr. Muntz and our scholarly cleric. There is an indefinable magnetism between him and the automobile, regardless of vintage, make, color, or condition. He detests small cars with a big man's scorn, but he will eye an ambulance, hearse, or nine passenger Cadillac with expert appraisal, as a Kentucky colonel scans horseflesh. He never pays more than a hundred and fifty dollars per car. But over the years he has driven a parade of vintage behemoths that change hands so rapidly I believe that he has seldom visited us twice in the same rig.

So complete is this gentle priest's thralldom to the machine, that he once bought a concrete mixer for ten dollars. It was regrettably half-filled with solid concrete, and he hauled it up to his little house in Indiana, with no further idea in mind than the pure joy of owning so much machinery. There is also parked on this property an old school bus, where Father sleeps when he has been too generous with invitations and finds his own room usurped by six children. In addition, there is a tractor, a wagon, a miniature train which he runs for the benefit of his friends' children, and two gasoline-driven gocarts. He loves having steel and motors and wheels nearby.

A man is best-known by his enthusiasms. Father Phil loves his church, the souls of mankind, Ireland, horses, books, tools and machinery, John McCormack, automobiles, Italian stogies, handball, swimming, and picnics involving one hundred people. He is an enthusiastic hater too. He hates television, movies, vegetables, salads, cocktail parties, and England. The stage of his activities shifts constantly, but is centered around Quigley Preparatory (where he teaches boys who call him the Great White Father), St. Malachy's rectory, a Negro parish (where he lives in an attic room with his roll-top desk, a chair propped up with an orange crate, and his books), and the farm in Indiana which is the joy of his heart.

The Indiana farm was acquired out of a need for some recreation that would give him respite from the routine of teaching. When he first laid eyes on it, the property consisted of forty acres of sandy soil, a little forest, and a three-room house which had fallen into an interesting state of disrepair that called forth every talent, tool and muscle he possessed. In the first week, a horse that had been tied up to the front porch took a notion to gallop away from a grasshopper, and in doing so, carried the front porch with him. Father Phil surveyed the situation and decided upon drastic action. He began to rebuild. Today, as a result of about fifteen years of arduously expended Thursdays (his day off from school), he has a house which contains a forty-foot living room, three bedrooms, a kitchen, a bathroom, and an enormous screened porch.

Father Phil has about twenty-four nephews and nieces of varying ages, and these have kept the farm occupied

and the fireplace well stocked with logs. And just about
every weekend in good weather there are picnics involving a goodly number of friends and relations. Father Phil
often turns the place over to families for their vacations
so that they have the pleasures of country living at least
once a year. The Christian Family Movement groups of
which he is chaplain hold family days there. The Pioneers,
a total-abstinence society out of Ireland, four hundred of
them, who also claim him as their chaplain, hold their
singularly dry diversions there—and these are balanced
by other groups of friends who bring their own beer. All
in all, the farm has a lived-in look.

It is undoubtedly due to this intense concentration of
gatherings that the main room of the farm gives at first
the impression of a secondhand furniture store. Leaning
next to the sofa is a posthole digger, several fence posts,
a spade, and a pickax. In another corner of the room is a
recording machine which apparently plays only tapes
of Irish music, and is accompanied periodically by the
sizzle of fried flies incautious enough to land on the
electric fly trap. Friends and relations have through the
years endowed Father Phil with their furniture mistakes
and upholstered horrors, and these now rest quite comfortably in the main room at the farm. He also cherishes
innumerable broken chairs, with the cane seats dripping
like lace, and what must be the first of the old round
dining room tables. Leering evilly from the ceiling rafters
is a huge fish mounted in about 1750 which had been
gathering dust in some basement before its rescue by
Father Phil. Strewn about are bathing suits, gym shoes to
fit any foot size, several saddles, coffee cups, and ashtrays
holding the relics of stogies. Nestled on high shelves along
the walls are cans of paint, rat poison, shellac, furniture

polish, machine oil, kerosene, insect bombs, and of course books.

I suspect that this epic confusion is due to a typically masculine rebellion against the world of womanly house-keepers who are constantly "tidying up" around the rectory. At any rate, it presents a bold challenge to the wives of the friends he invites to relax at the farm. The ladies always spend two or three hours straightening up before they sit down to enjoy their visit.

Father Phil visited Ireland, land of his dreams, a few years back. He found no fault in the lovely isle, and stanchly maintains he found it true to tradition—a veritable paradise on earth. When asked if he had gone to Europe as well, he responded with genuine surprise:

"What for? Ireland is the only place on earth worth the trouble of traveling to see." He intends to go back at the first opportunity.

Father Phil is a complete teetotaler, dedicated to the ideals of the Pioneers, that of total abstinence from alcoholic beverages in reparation to the Sacred Heart for the sins of drunkenness. Some years ago on the way down to Quigley, Father saw a bad accident, and drawing over to the curb, ran to the assistance of a man who was so badly hurt that Father gave him absolution. When the police came and removed him to a hospital, Father went along, just to make sure everything possible would be done for the poor fellow. Unfortunately, the man died, and Father went on his way, thankful at least that he had prepared the man to meet his God. About a month later he received a call at the rectory from the man's widow. She had been trying in vain to find the unknown priest who had done such a wonderful service for her husband, and only lately had she been able to trace him down.

"I'm going to send you something in appreciation, Father," said the woman. Father protested that this was his pleasure and duty, and that no further thanks were called for. The woman insisted.

Sure enough, a week later, a package was delivered to Father Phil at the rectory. It was a case of very good Scotch.

The Family Next Door

Neighbors, says CFM's Yellow Book, have a right to our help, sympathy, and love. Christ and His Church have always taught this; and today, in a straightforward, practical manner, the neighbors of Christian Family Movement couples are experiencing the effects of this ancient doctrine restated in modern, dynamic action.

The evening we were introduced to the Yellow Book and began to discuss neighbors, Al and I exchanged one of those eloquent looks that are the special means of private communication between married people.

"I wonder if they ever had neighbors like—" said Al to me, wordlessly.

"I know," I interrupted soundlessly, "the Blythes—no, they couldn't have!"

And we leaned back and allowed our eyes to glaze over while our memory took us back to the early days of our marriage, when we spent an entire year and a half in the clutches of Fifty Little Fingers.

We had been married about two years, and had our first baby, little Ann. The third floor apartment became a prison when spring came. There was no place to get the baby into the sun; so we went out and bought a little bungalow in a neighborhood of small homes and miles of prairie.

The day we moved in, we met the Blythe family. Mrs. Blythe came in to welcome us, and apologize for the broken glass. Her merry brood had broken nineteen of our

windows; the glass was still sticking in the fresh varnish
of the bedroom floors. Mr. Blythe would replace them
that afternoon, she smiled. The children had been punished, of course. She had called the police. Her father, a
police captain, had driven up in the squad car (the children loved the siren), and had given them a good
scolding.

"You know how children are," she said, indulgently,
"they love to hear the sound of breaking glass."

That afternoon, Mr. Blythe came and installed the new
windows with a skill born of long practice. He announced
himself ready and willing to be of service at any time, and
we timidly ventured the hope that no further window
work would be necessary.

A day or two later, I went into the back yard to begin
the sunning we had so long sought for young Ann. The
yard was fenced in with an empty lot on one side, and the
Blythe's yard on the other. I've never seen a yard quite
like theirs. Mr. Blythe, obviously fed up with trying to
grow grass, had his entire yard area covered with gravel.
In the center of this wasteland stood a playground sized
gym set, as high as their second floor windows. It had
obviously been purchased from a school district. It had
ladders, steel slides, swings, gym bars and steel rings a
good six feet off the gravel. There were five children in
the yard in various stages of undress, down to a cherubic
toddler completely unclothed. In and out of the children's
legs swarmed a flock of very sick chickens; some with
large, painfully denuded areas on their backs, and others
with no feathers at all. A board ramp leading to the basement window suggested where these fowl were housed;
and the amount of loose gravel stone in *our* yard suggested

how the Blythe clan amused itself when the delights of the giant gym equipment palled.

One by one the children introduced themselves; I'll say this for the Blythes: they had impressive names. There were Percival, Anastasia, Ernest, Bruce, and Westlock. (Westlock was the unclothed member.) Anastasia was the only girl, poor child, and was trying hard to take care of the smaller ones. I suggested that she get some pants for Westlock and she immediately picked up a pair of jeans and thrust him into them.

"He'll have 'em off in five minutes," she predicted, accurately. Mother, she confided, was at school. She was taking courses in child psychology which necessitated her absence from home several mornings a week, when Anastasia would be pressed into service as baby sitter.

Al ventured a question.

"What's wrong with those chickens?"

Percival said Daddy was still reading up on it, and had not as yet come up with answers. Al went off to work and left me with Ann in the yard. She was in a playpen, and after moving it as far out of throwing range as I could, I went in to do more unpacking. Every little while I'd peek out to make sure all was well.

I began unpacking wedding presents we had never had space for in the apartment when I heard a scream that hit my ears like a blow. It was Ann. Racing to the yard I saw an empty playpen and almost died of panic trying to locate the screams. Then I saw her. Ernest and Percival had her perched on top of the trapeze; upon spotting me they were beating a hasty retreat. Ann was clutching the bars in terror and was almost blue with fright. I don't know how I got over there—I must have jumped the fence. I remember climbing up that slippery steel ladder

and trying to call reassurances to her and wondering how I'd ever get her down to safety.

When I reached her, she flung her arms around my neck so tightly we both almost fell, but our angels must have been on special guard that day. As I came down the ladder again, trying to watch my footing and comfort the sobbing baby, I found myself on a level with the Blythe kitchen window, and looking into the bright eyes of Mrs. Blythe, who was having coffee after her morning class at

school. She eyed me with interest. I guess she thought I
had come over to play on the trapeze.

"Did you see what your boys did to my baby?" I inquired at the top of my lungs.

She smiled deprecatingly.

"No, I missed this one—but they sure do think up some
dillies, those kids." This was delivered with a mixture of
pride and objectivity. I retired from the field in defeat.

When we went to the parish rectory to register, we told
the pastor our name and address. As he copied them down
he wore a bemused air, as if wresting with an impulse.

"Let's see—you live right next door to the Blythe's,
then."

We dumbly nodded, and he hesitated, then leaned
over the desk with intense interest.

"Tell me," he asked, "did you *buy* that house?" We admitted that we had.

"Do you know you're the fifth family in that house in
less than three years?" This was news to us, but we were
already aware of a reason as to why this should be so.

He, too, was trying hard to be objective.

"Interesting family, really. Loads of pep and imagination. Need a lot of space, those kids—plenty of room to
run." But as he spoke I detected a glint of steel coming
into his eye as he related what he termed grimly "their
latest." The school had recently held a paper drive, net-
ting something like fourteen tons of newspaper and magazines that had all been wrapped and stored in an unused
portable school room, awaiting the trucks that would cart
them away. The Blythe kids had broken in one Saturday
morning and spent the day there, systematically unwrap-
ping and scattering each bundle looking for comic books.

It took the sisters three days to retie the bundles of paper so the truckers would agree to haul them away.

"Give them plenty of room" was his parting advice to us.

We had come to a similar conclusion, but found them impossible to avoid. They were as friendly as puppies and infinitely more destructive. And they had an insatiable curiosity about us, and the queer way we lived.

Father Lord came to visit and bless the house. We had finished dinner and he walked into the living room and sat down to play the piano. We were relaxed and happy in the prospect of a delightful session of music. Father knew the songs from every musical show since 1900 and played them with a zest and joy that could charm the birds from the trees. This time, however, it was Blythes he charmed. I noted with concern that they had all taken their accustomed positions in the tree outside the front window, and were swaying happily to the music. But as Westlock was in his usual state of dishabille, I was stricken with a bride's fear of impropriety and sent Al out quietly to ask them to retire to a tree on their home grounds. They swarmed down as silently as Indians and I was congratulating myself that Father hadn't even noticed them when around the open windows came small hands quietly gripping each sill. Ten hands; and just behind each set a pair of piercing blue eyes. I held my breath and motioned to Al, but he was now singing, and there was nothing to do but sit there and stare at the fifty little fingers and wonder how long they could chin themselves that way.

Father found them, of course, and roared with laughter. He insisted that they all come in for ice cream, reasonably imposing a condition that Westlock first don a pair of pants. The Blythes and Father Lord had a glorious evening.

World War II was in progress, and in all the vacant lots around the neighborhood little Victory gardens bloomed; row upon row of radishes, carrots, green beans, peas, tomatoes, and corn. At the end of our street were three lots tended by a Polish family, a German family, and the Blythes. The first two gardens were beautifully cultivated in neat green rows. The third was unusual. The Blythes decided to concentrate on two items: tomatoes and cabbages.

They planted one hundred tomato plants and seeded the remainder of the lot with cabbages. They went all out for the garden with bright new garden tools for all the children, transported each afternoon in a big green wheelbarrow. They marched in procession past our house each afternoon to work on their garden. It was a year of great abundance. Their one hundred tomato plants gave forth thousands of tomatoes and all in the same week. There must have been five hundred cabbages squatting luxuriously on the rich prairie loam. But there was a definite limit to the Blythe gastronomic capacity for these comestibles; the thousands of tomatoes were hardly dented by the ordinary salad usage.

As for the cabbages, it turned out that no one in the family had ever liked cabbage, so after the neighbors on the block were given ten apiece, the available market was glutted and the rest were allowed to rot where they stood. The stench on those hot summer days became unbearable, and the bugs from the perishing crop made short work of the other two gardens. Bushels of overripe tomatoes stood in rows on the Blythe back porch, and the question of prompt disposal became a great matter for discussion. Canning, it appeared, was out of the question because of the work involved. One evening the procession passed the house again, this time armed with kerosene and matches and shovels. Gathering up the too bountiful harvest of cabbages, they poured kerosene on it and it burned like an ancient holocaust.

The tomatoes still plagued them. A neighbor down the block had just painted his front door a glistening white when the Blythes happened by with a wagonload of overripe tomatoes. They apparently got a great delight from the sound of tomatoes slapping against wet paint. This satisfactorily removed the tomato surplus but got them in trouble with the neighbor, who was inclined to be a bit stuffy about the deed. Mr. Blythe confided to Al that he believed that there was an active persecution of his children going on in the area. Sometime later, when Ernest and Bruce dropped half a pound of marshmallow cookies down Mr. Blythe's automobile gas tank, we knew from the commotion that issued from their house that Mr. Blythe was beginning to side with the rest of the neighbors.

Percival set fire to Chez Blythe one morning when the lady of the house was at school, and told interested firemen that he was sure glad the fire hadn't reached the attic where his thoughtful daddy had stored barrels of sugar. Fire fascinated these youngsters, their mother said.

We stuck it out for a year and a half; and, secure in the knowledge that our endurance record was thus far unchallenged, sold the house.

The family who bought it had four powerful looking teenaged sons who looked as though they could take care of themselves. We left without a qualm and have never gone back.

Since then we have been blessed with marvelous neighbors whose virtues shine in the light of vivid comparison. We can't help wondering, at times, what a CFM couple living next to the Blythe family would have done in our shoes. It's one of those things I file away under "mysteries."

Morning Madness

Ben Franklin was undoubtedly a wise man, and I suspect that no small part of this wisdom derives from his having latched onto a universal truth at a comparatively youthful age. For it is strangely true that almost any statement, no matter how ridiculous, will be unquestioningly accepted, provided it is stated in verse.

When I consider that one about "Early to bed and early to rise, / Makes a man healthy, wealthy, and wise," I think I know why the collection of these gems was called *Poor Richard's Almanac*. Poor Richard, indeed! Early rising in our household, practiced for a scant six weeks, has increased our expenditures, frayed my already languishing nerves, worn new paths on the furniture, caused several costly plumbing bills, strained my tired washing machine to audible squeaking protests, and depleted the family supply of wearing apparel to that awesome state where everything needs replacing at the same time.

I shouldn't complain, because, like the puppy that grew into the most detestable animal on earth, and the camping trip when everyone got earaches, it was all my idea in the first place. I had been quietly arising at 6 A.M., that sacred time of morning when the air is fresh and the sky full of promise of a glorious new day. I had joined the little group at the six-thirty Mass each morning, and found a whole new world. Walking down deserted streets, bird-watching along the way, becoming acquainted with the neighborhood complement of squirrels and rabbits,

and nodding to the dear old ladies I had never met at the
Parents' Nights, I delighted in this quiet time of the day.
At Mass I could thank God for all His rich blessings;
decide what chores I would accomplish, and sandwich
in a few petitions as I participated in the liturgy. At home
by ten after seven, there was time to throw a load of
clothes in the washing machine, whip the living room
into order and empty the dishwasher before calling the
family for breakfast. A thoroughly satisfying start.

Summer vacation came, and after my husband departed
for the office, there were five slugabeds upstairs, snoozing
through the beautiful morning, and drifting down around
ten-thirty, foraging for breakfast just as I was ready to do
the windows. I tiptoed through my mornings for several
weeks, taking pity on the minds worn out from the yearly
struggle with geometry, physics, history, and fractions.
It finally dawned on me that the grades they had pulled
hadn't called for a great deal of effort on their part. And
one morning, as I tried to muffle the sound of the vacuum
cleaner, I got an idea. Gathering my young about me at
dinnertime that evening, I spoke as follows:

"Youth," quoth I, "you are all missing the best time
of the day by sleeping late in the morning! Beginning
with tomorrow, you will arise at a given signal, dress,
make your beds, and report down for breakfast with
Daddy. When the dishes are done, you will be assigned
tasks to do which will prevent some of the silver threads
among the gold, and will also learn skills which will undoubtedly enrich your lives. By nine-thirty, you will find
yourselves free to do whatever you like, comforted by
the thought that you have pulled your share of the load."
I immediately began to sing:

onslaught of tuition bills were being dwindled away to the coffers of the Chicago Transit Authority and similarly wealthy companies. Their clothing was shot. And worst of all, they were running out of ideas. Any day now, I thought, one of them was bound to suggest building a fort in the back yard, or a tree house. I was in no condition to stand it.

It was cowardly of me, I know, but I never admitted I was wrong. I just didn't call them next morning. They lay upstairs sleeping quietly just like all of their friends. The freshly ironed clothing was still fresh at dinnertime. The cold meat in the refrigerator lasted until next shopping day. I buzzed through the housework with a minimum of noise, leaving the bedrooms for them to tidy when they awoke around 11 A.M. Their friends began calling around 1 P.M, and found their erstwhile companions bright-eyed and eager for the day. So what if it's a short day? Growing children need plenty of rest.

The Man in the Lake

In a city of Chicago's size, it is evident that not a few of the incidents that make up its daily life will be of a tragic nature. Though my childhood and youth were happily free of the recollection of tragedy—which may be indicative of the providential care with which we were surrounded, or a bad memory, I can't be sure which—when I was older there were plenty of opportunities for acquaintance with sorrow and death.

One day my husband and I took our children for a brisk walk along the lake in the early fall, and came face to face with horror. The wind was strong, and already suggestive of the icy blasts soon to come. The children all wore heavy jackets, and raced along the shore to the accompaniment of our cautions about getting too near the edge. The steely gray sky over the lake began to darken, and I had begun to shake with chill; we were preparing to walk back to the car when we saw him.

Wearing only light summer clothing, he walked into the water, and when he continued walking right into the icy lake, we were too stunned to move. My husband worriedly rounded up the children, fearing he knew not what. The man was about waist-deep when we realized that he had no intention of stopping; he was going to drown himself before our eyes. The children began to look anxiously at us, and ask what he was doing. My husband told me to keep them together, he was going to try to get a policeman. So we sat helplessly down on the embankment, huddled together for warmth, and the youngest began to cry.

I had a rosary, and told the children that we were going to pray for the poor man, who was probably very sick and needed help. We began the Rosary together, the children awed and serious.

As we got to the third decade, my husband and a policeman came running along the shore. The policeman had wisely called the Coast Guard, who were cruising on the other side of Navy Pier; meantime, he decided to try to reach the man, who by this time was just a little speck in the dark water. The man seemed to be staring up at the clouds. The policeman stripped to his underwear, and dove in, while chills shivered down our spines at the thought of how cold that water must be. He swam rapidly, but the man must have seen him coming, for he disappeared beneath the surface. The policeman was unable to find him, and after an agonizing search, came out again.

The Coast Guard cutter finally retrieved the body of the poor man and brought it up on shore. By this time a little crowd of onlookers had gathered, and our youngest child suddenly shouted with excitement that a priest was coming. Miraculously, there he was, running along the shore toward the crowd. By the time my husband and I had joined the group, he was bending over the man, giving him conditional absolution. The last thing I heard as I turned quickly away was the bitter voice of a woman who had just come up.

"What does he think he's going to do anyway? He can't bring the poor guy back to life with that hocus-pocus!"

And then I remembered that she might be wrong. There's every chance that's just what the priest had been doing; bringing the poor, despairing, crazed man back to Life.

The Health Kick

Women are great learners. It is difficult to leaf through a woman's magazine without finding one or more articles titled "How To Do . . ." anything from using that attic space for a sewing room to weaving rugs out of discarded hose. Behind every adult education class is the assurance that 95 per cent of the pupils will be women who want to learn Russian, typing, dramatic art, jewelry crafting, upholstering, or effective speaking. I have yet to meet a woman whose eyes didn't glaze over as she wistfully remarked, "As soon as the children are grown, I'm going to learn how to make hats—or paintings." I think it all stems from our basic conviction that the world is so full of a number of things that we would all be happy as kings—provided we could learn how to *do* some of these things. Whatever this urge be traced to—and I can just hear the psychologists deciding that this is an urge based on a desire for greater security—women, anyway, can be talked into practically anything that might come under the general heading of self-improvement, of the improvement of the home.

I offer all of the foregoing in the hope that it will at least partially explain the madness that descended upon me about five years ago, when I succumbed to the spell of a lady nutritionist. She had written a book expounding a theory of food selection and preparation which involved a complete about-face from our usually comfortable eating habits. By the time I had come to the end of the first chapter I was gravely panicky about what refined sugars and flour had already wrought upon the defenseless children I had been feeding, particularly since the author laid heavy stress upon a rather nasty fact. So deleted in food values had our refined flours become, in comparison with the whole-grained products our forefathers fought Indians on, that even the vermin refused to infest them when they were stored. Even the addition of vitamins, so highly touted in advertisements of bread, was deceptive, since the manufacturers had taken away 100 per cent of the value and restored only about 30 per cent. By the time the book had fallen from my nerveless fingers there was a fire in my eye and a new vocabulary on my lips.

"Brewers' yeast," I said succinctly.

"Huh?" commented my husband.

"Brewers' yeast, blackstrap molasses, yogurt, and wheat germ."

My husband looked puzzled, and vaguely worried.

"From this moment on," cried I, passionately, "I will feed my family foods which will build health! I shall cease pouring their eyesight and strong bones down the drain with the vegetable water!"

My husband asked simply, "What's that book you're reading?" But I was no longer there. I was in the pantry clearing out the cake mixes, pizza mixes, pie mixes, and coffeecake, waffle, and pancake mixes. There was only a little white sugar left, so I allowed that to remain. The jellies and jams I moved to the top shelf so I wouldn't cringe every time I opened the cabinet. I seldom buy canned goods anyway, preferring frozen, but I made a mental note to use only fresh food in season, if possible. Then I went to work on the menus for the coming week.

They leaned heavily to meats such as liver rolled in wheat germ, and kidney creole.

One of the best indications of a healthy and hearty childhood is its adaptability to the wild-eyed experiments of amateur parents. Children have submitted to vacations spent visiting historical sites, and learned the Morse code during dinner; they have learned to use "your very own" silverware, drinking glass, or hand towel, depending upon which issue of *Good Housekeeping* mother is reading; and I am personally acquainted with children who actually brush their teeth *voluntarily* after every meal. There is no end to the amiability of a healthy child.

And so when the dietary revolution swung into effect, I anticipated no real difficulty, having taken that elementary precaution of convincing my spouse that this was dogma and any deviation should be looked at in the light of the long-range view, which was the ultimate good health (physical and mental) of our gravest responsibility in this life, our children.

Halfway measures do not interest me. In fact, they never even occur to me. I am a wall-to-wall, all or nothing person. And so, having found the nearest diet store, and having purchased the necessary ingredients for the strong bones, teeth, blood, and muscle (I had half an idea that good food might even improve the mathematical deficiencies in our brood), I served the first meal of the new era. It consisted, as I recall, of the liver rolled in wheat germ, three vegetables (two green and one yellow) all cooked so lightly that they retained a crunchy quality, milk, to which had been added secret ingredients, and for dessert, fresh peaches. A certain amount of psychological conditioning had been done before the meal by my husband, in the form of vague promises of swift action following

any adverse comment. Nevertheless the comments were rather striking in their clear-cut unanimity, though there was a divergence of opinion as to which was the most detestable of the dishes I had prepared.

The next day, afire with apostolic fervor, I phoned several friends and suggested that they read the book and see if they, too, did not wish to reform. My mother, I recall now, murmured something in a gentle tone about taking no thought for food or drink, and reminded me to consider the lilies of the field; but I was too far gone for spiritual considerations. My brother Tom, a doctor, strangely unmoved by my impassioned denunciation of the food producers of America, held out for what he called the common-sense approach to nutrition.

A month of healthful eating passed in some fashion, and my husband began to suffer stomach pains. He had been harboring an incipient ulcer for years, and when it now developed into a painful condition, I accompanied him (over his dead body) to the doctor. The doctor examined him carefully, and said he had an ulcer. This kind of thing drives my husband crazy.

"I've had an ulcer for years, Doctor," he said with frightening civility. "What I want to know is, what can I do about it?"

"To control the pain, diet is the first thing necessary, of course," began the doctor. And here I broke in in ready agreement.

"That's just what I've been telling him, Doctor, and I've certainly been giving my family a healthful diet this past month: wheat germ, blackstrap molasses, plenty of fresh vegetables and fruits. . . ."

The doctor turned his full attention on me in flattering intensity. "That's fine, Mrs. Anton," he said gravely. "Why didn't you try arsenic?"

And so, one more great idea bit the dust. My husband was coddled back to bloom with plenty of cottage cheese, strained baby foods, and soft white bread. The menu at Chez Anton went back to its proper place in the scheme of things. The children still hate vegetables, but they come by it honestly. It runs in both families.

The Ironing of It All

Has anyone noticed how fashionable it has become, at dinner parties and PTA meetings, to speak archly about current social trends? Overnight, it seems to me, everyone has become enamored of the social significance of everything from electric toothbrushes to a frightening development termed electronic music. My friends have their fingers on the pulse, so to speak, and are succinct on subjects that even include gentle surmises as to whether IBM was overpriced to begin with. But they carefully avoid, I've noticed, the most crucial problem of our times: namely, what in heaven's name has happened to that triumphant state of soul attainable only through the knowledge that the ironing for the week has been finished?

The gruesome fact is that lurking in almost every laundry room in America is a pile of unironed clothing. Talk to any woman you meet. Ask her if her ironing is finished. Ignore, if you can, the flashing light of mayhem in her eye. You will discover that, unless she lives alone, she has a backlog of ironing that may date from last week to as far back as last summer. In a family containing growing children, the laundry room will almost certainly contain a minor mountain of unfinished ironing that never really changes shape—just contents.

Homemakers are not lazy. They work harder than the previous generation to attain homes that are attractive, clean, and inviting. Their own appearance speaks of good grooming and an inbred clothes-sense. They entertain more, attend more meetings, and have more children than their mothers had. But their ironing is never finished.

Ironing has become a treadmill task, the end of which is forever out of sight. I submit that this unhappy bulge in the laundry room is the direct result of the invention of the automatic washer and dryer.

Now don't misunderstand. When these "laborsaving" devices were invented, I was the first in line. I have a long memory, and still wince at the remembered back-ache of "wash day," commonly the first day of the week, otherwise known as "Blue Monday." Gathering up the family wash and descending to the Black Hole of Calcutta to sort, bleach, starch, wash, rinse, wring, and finally hang out (after stringing up a clothesline in the yard) the week's supply of sheets, pillowcases, towels, table-cloths, shirts, and the intimate assortment of clothing for a family was a job that took until nearly 2 P.M. Then, if it didn't rain, or the line didn't break, the clothes could be retrieved when dry. The clothespins were collected back into the clothespin bag, the line was taken down again and stored, and the clothes were sorted and folded ready for "ironing day," which was Tuesday.

"Ironing day" was another fun day, but as the last freshly pressed dress or shirt was carried up to the second floor, and one collapsed, sobbing, on the bed, the conso-lation that dried those tears was the realization that six days would blissfully pass before the ordeal by water had to be undergone again.

So what happened? Someone decided to lighten the burden. At a cost of nearly five times what the old wash-ing machine was worth, we could now buy an automatic washing machine and dryer. The housewife bought the idea immediately, and began getting fitted for a bowling ball and brushing up on her bridge.

But no sooner had the machines entered the house when another social change emerged which I shall characterize by the term "the white socks syndrome." Suddenly, every child in the nation began wearing white socks! Not only the girls, but, incredibly, the boys. And those socks were bulky items, worn with loafers which left a dark brown stain on the soles of the socks.

This universal trafficking in socks made itself felt in the American home. The first change was a kind of oriental impulse which laid hold of our youth; they began removing their shoes upon entering the house. The rugs and carpeting benefited, for the outside dirt was now resting on the soles of the twelve or fourteen loafers in the front hall. Another change was the soaring accident rate, in response to the hazards encountered in darkened front hallways. The most significant change was the constant changing of socks. But who cared? After all, there was an automatic machine in the basement, and washing involved no wear or tear on anyone.

A new pattern began to emerge. While upstairs changing to clean white socks, it was but a simple matter to change as well the easily washable shorts and blouse for a fresher, brighter outfit. The discarded clothing was neatly dropped into the hamper. By now the balance of nature had been tampered with, and everyone knows what that means! I think it safe to state that from the day the washing machine was automated no one ever spent an entire day in the same clothing he donned in the morning. Everything was washable (dry cleaning was reserved for Daddy's suits, Mother's best dresses, and the draperies), so into the hamper it went. When I had to buy a second hamper, I began to realize that I was a functioning part of a significant social revolution.

"Toss it in the hamper" became its theme. I began emptying the hamper daily. I could blithely throw a load into my trusty little automatic machine and go about my other work without waiting for the cycle to complete. When the load was washed, rinsed, and wrung, it shut off automatically. On the next trip to the basement, I would fill the dryer, adjust the timer, put another load in the washer, and so on. Finally this trip became so habitual that "wash day" disappeared into oblivion.

What happened was every day became wash day. Now each time I descend to the basement to change a fuse, find a light bulb, or store a blanket, I throw a load into the washing machine and transfer the washed clothing into the dryer. Christmas, Easter, or Fourth of July, dressed for the evening, or hatted and gloved for Mass on Sunday, I falter not in the constant, everlastingly unfinished washing-machine bit.

The gigantic soap interests have gone a long way toward making it all sound like great fun. Words, like "ease" and "gracious living" and "soft, lovely white hands," all of which used to characterize the idle rich, are now used to describe the salubrious effects of laundry soap. And the suds! Every river and stream in the land is foaming with detergents and longlasting suds that have floated the soil out of the clothes and have just gone on floating.

With washing now a daily rather than a weekly task, and the amount of clothing worked on increased sevenfold, it takes the agile mind but a moment to conclude that this increase will be reflected in the ironing as well; for what is washed must be ironed.

And the bitterly truthful fact is, that no one has yet

come up with anything that can make the ironing of it all any easier. There is, indeed, seven times more ironing today than our mothers had.

For a while it looked as though the fabric interests had the problem licked. To date, however, the "Drip-Dry" label means little more than just that—the clothes will drip, and eventually dry. You still have to iron them. Clothing that is "Drip-Dry" falls into three categories:

1. Nylon hose. These dry with spectacular ease and efficiency. Overnight, instead of three days as of yore.

2. "Drip-Dry" cottons clearly marked "'Hand wash'; *DO NOT PLACE IN AUTOMATIC DRYER!"* This, of course, means that you must again return to the primitive state. These articles must be washed in the laundry tub by hand, and then hung up dripping wet (do not wring) and gently worked into shape while they are drying, so as to eliminate ironing. This not only involves a drainage system in the laundry room, but a mopping up procedure. All in all, ironing would be easier.

3. Miracle fabrics that can be machine-washed and machine-dried and need what is euphemistically called "just a touch" of ironing. Freely translated, this means, "you'll have to iron it if you want to wear it, and if you get the iron *too hot* it will melt the fabric."

We live, perhaps, in a transitional period of some sort. Science may at this very moment be working on the solution to this problem of the mountain of ironing. I sincerely hope so, because unless the habit of ironing becomes as compulsive as the habit of washing, there will have to be remodeling done in most laundry rooms. Some of my friends boast that they'd rather store clean clothes (the ironing mountain) than dirty ones. But I can recall a past in which the clean clothing was kept upstairs in closets and dresser drawers.

And now, if you'll excuse me, there are about seven blouses I must search for in the pile of ironing. They're each marked "needs no ironing," so the job shouldn't take more than two hours. Which reminds me of Sylvia, proprietor of the local linen shop where I recently purchased a bedspread and draperies. They were all clearly marked "washable," and I noted this fact aloud with pleasure. Sylvia set me straight in a hurry.

"Darling, take a tip. When anything is marked 'washable,' *send it to the cleaner!* It'll turn out much nicer!"

Owen

One good way to teach responsibility to children is to allow them to have a pet, the experts agree. When I tell you that there was a particularly hectic period during which we harbored goldfish, a hamster, a cat, a dog, a Belgian hare, and a parakeet, you will understand the lengths to which we were prepared to go to achieve this value in our young. Of course, we hadn't intended it that way. They just all decided on a different pet. Billy had two.

Only time will tell whether the desirable trait of character was achieved, but the experience left their father and me with a distinct allergy to animals.

In a long and painful memory of animal guests at Chez Anton, several dogs stand out in heroic bas-relief, so that one is hard put to decide which is deserving of the greatest detestation. I think my husband would agree that it's a tossup between Daisy and Owen, with Owen having an outside edge.

Owen came to us, believe it or not, by train all the way from Washington, D.C. A friend at a naval hospital there took pity on the gorgeous beast, because he was due to be used experimentally, and it seemed a terrible waste of dog flesh. So he called us long-distance, and begged us to offer Owen a home and loving care. Being very young, we thought he'd make a nice pet. We told him to send him on, we'd meet him at the station. And so we met Owen. He was beautiful, big and black, with a pedigree that went back to the golden age of Labrador retrievers and a will that made the conquistadors look like Milquetoasts.

Our first task, stunningly indicated in the arrogant behavior of our guest, was to attempt to train him. Housebreaking him was not necessary, since that talent had already been developed by some unknown hero in his past. What we wished to accomplish was a far more simple task: that of making Owen respond to his name and trot obediently up to us when called. It proved hopeless. Al had trained at least twenty dogs in his lifetime, but he failed miserably with Owen. My will was infinitely weaker than the dog's, so I got nowhere either. But living with a beast the proportions of Owen made obedience absolutely necessary. We had to train him or desert him. We chose the expensive solution. We turned him over to Cal's Private School for Dogs, an educational establishment which promised a diploma with honors at the end of an eight-week course.

We visited Owen on Sunday afternoons for "owner orientation periods." Cal's method proved strikingly simple. He turned Owen into a large, fenced yard, and let him run free. Then he would sharply call "Here Owen!" in a tone that brooked no nonsense. Owen, true to his aristocratic blood, ignored the summons, whereupon Cal took a bead on him with a slingshot and unerringly clipped our friend near the tail. Owen leaped three feet into the air, but when he came down, he trotted over to Svengali and sat at his feet, eying him expectantly. Cal fed him some candy and patted him on the head.

We watched this process for a while, and went home in a state of puzzlement. The slingshot method might work for Cal, but I knew I would never be able to aim that well. As it turned out, I didn't have to use a slingshot.

Owen learned to respond to any sharp, loud noise, and we found in subsequent visits that he was now answering to his name when uttered in conjunction with a retort from an air rifle fired into the air.

Graduation day, at the end of the eight-week period, was fittingly simple and dignified. Owen had been groomed to his toe nails and shone like burnished tar; his noble head erect, panting in attentive appreciation as Cal delivered the baccalaureate address. Cal's manner, I thought, was proper to the ceremony. He spoke in low, solemn tones, his voiced tinged with something bordering on wistfulness. He urged us on to yet greater heights in our fight for the upper hand with Owen. Nothing, he said, is more rewarding or splendid than a dog that has been well trained. And with a valedictorian quiver in his voice, he told us that Owen had just barely gotten through; our dog had not passed *cum laude*. He was, said Cal, somewhat testily eying the magnificent Owen, a clown; and he added as an afterthought that a vital part was missing from what ought to have been an adequate supply of brains. I began to suspect that we had not been in time to save Owen from scientific experimentation after all. And so we bore the scholar home.

We lived in a quiet neighborhood. I sometimes think with dismay about what must have been the consensus of neighborhood opinion about our little household. Consider that each morning, perforce, we had to let our pet outside, and that the only means at our disposal to get him to return to roost was to go out on the front porch with an air rifle, call his name loudly, and fire a blank shot into the air. Owen made quite a sight, bounding across the victory gardens, his magnificent black tail straight out behind him, his tongue hanging out as he obeyed his master's summons in a final burst of speed.

He learned absolutely nothing else. Inhibited by a sense of the fitness of things, we never attempted to use the rifle indoors, so Owen had things pretty much his own way once he regained the privacy of his home. He would neither lie down, sit up, beg, or stay out of the living room like the dogs belonging to all of our friends. We were embarrassed by his dominion over the family.

Father Cahill, that intrepid tamer of animals large and small (he had just completed a horse-training course by correspondence), undertook to teach Owen to sit upon command. After all, it was a small house, and with Owen standing around, the living room seemed overcrowded. Father placed two giant, confident hands upon Owen's silken back, and exerted firm pressure downward while repeating the words "Sit, Owen." But Owen, locking his kneecaps in a viselike stance, remained standing. One entire month saw this pitiful scene repeated almost nightly, with Father Cahill finally throwing in the sponge.

"That is no dog," he stated balefully, massaging his aching arms, "that is a mule." But Owen's bark left little room for doubt as to his canine heritage. He barked loud and long, by day and night. No burglar would have ventured across our property line, even if we had kept our silver on the front porch. Owen's bark sounded like Leo, the M-G-M lion, with a bad cold.

But human beings can accustom themselves to almost anything. In time we learned to tolerate Owen and his overpowering presence in our living room. Just as he was at last showing some signs of civility, we moved.

This upset Owen completely. He grew morose and moody. Finally even the rifle couldn't win him back. Tea

rooms and butcher shops began calling us daily. The conversation always began:

"Say, is this your dog—a big black one?" We began paying out rewards for his return, only to have him take off again the next day.

Finally Al gave up. "Owen," he said one evening, removing the identifying dog collar, "I have paid out my last cent for your ransom. I shall now open the front door. If you do not come back, it is all right with me." With these words, he opened wide the door. We never saw Owen again. There were tales, for months later, about a hound in the neighborhood destroying flower beds and frightening the natives out of their wits. We kept our mouths shut. We knew someone would take in this beautiful dog and give him a home.

Owen and his education provided conversational material for years. I recall vividly sitting in the Imperial House at an elegant little dinner with Al's employer and his wife. I launched confidently into the saga of Owen, undaunted by my husband's nervous little grimaces and under-the-table nudgings. It was only when I came to Cal's succinct statement about Owen's mental capacity that I was struck by the peculiar coincidence that my husband had been vainly trying to call to my attention. His employer's first name is Owen.

That Look

I suppose it is natural that in an age like ours which glorifies trifles, the solid virtues elude us. The mixture becomes so rich that fat forms on top, and we can't fish out the meat, but keep coming up with noodles. The wonderful network of communication between men—newspapers, radio, and television—no longer communicates much of great value, having sold itself to commercial interests which tell us not how to live wisely, but what to buy.

Perhaps this accounts for the fact that people have begun to buy spiritual books again; average people who are fed up with dissertations on "tired blood" and "stupendous bargains." Ordinary men long for God. And once one is convinced that life is essentially a spiritual journey, the logical first step is to find a pilot, a spiritual director.

Some time ago, when this decision crystallized for me, I found a spiritual director. God has always been very good to me. He sent me a wonderful husband, five wonderful children, and a powerful yearning for heaven in spite of them. One of the first things my spiritual director taught me was that getting to heaven was not going to be accomplished in spite of them at all; but rather with them, and because of them. He has made it embarrassingly clear that the only thing that stands in my way is *me*. This is the sort of "hard saying" that I hate to hear. Most women do. And it doesn't make it any easier that a man has to point it out.

My spiritual director is an interesting person. He combines the best features of Galahad, the Curé of Ars, and Groucho Marx. He talks like a Dutch uncle, with overtones of Harry the Horse. The only trouble is, he's German, while I am of Irish descent. And the virtues he has decided to help me gain are all German virtues, utterly alien to me. Prudence (this is his special pet) and humility, and, I believe, though he's never come right out and said it, thrift. Some years ago, when my own extravagance overwhelmed me, I confessed it to a priest and awaited my penance fearfully. From the grill came the soothing tones of a big Irish voice which said:

"Well now, that doesn't sound so bad at all, at all." He must have been a visiting missionary or something. I've searched in vain for him all these years, but he's gone.

My S.D.'s name ends in S.J. His love for the Society of Jesus is deep and profound. His favorite prayers are two: the lovely prayer of St. Ignatius which begins "Lord make me generous in Thy service . . ." and the second one is a heartfelt prayer of thanksgiving: "Thank God I never married" is the way he phrases it.

Father had an operation not long ago. Unwilling to have him whisked to his reward before I could get a toehold on the first plateau (see *Seven Storey Mountain*), I selfishly sent out a call for prayers on his behalf that rivaled the Bishop's Relief Drive in scope and results. The school children prayed in three separate schools; the sisters prayed in their chapels; my friends all hauled themselves over to early Mass on the day of the operation while I alternated between Mass and endless Rosaries.

When it was all over, I tiptoed to the hospital to see him. I found him propped up in bed, wearing a surprisingly debonair robe with tricky designs on it, scowling at a newspaper.

"How did it go, Father," I whispered, my eyes brimming with tears of relief.

"Fine," he said briskly. "Incision's so small they've put a Band-Aid on it—I've been walking all over the hospital." I couldn't help but feel apologetic to heaven for the avalanche of prayers over so apparently trivial a matter. Then I realized that this rapid recovery was exactly what we had all been praying for. Father put the paper in his lap and fixed me with a look punctuated by one raised eyebrow.

"Are you aware," he said, with the air of a man suddenly blessed with new insight into mystery, "that women are now putting paint on their eyes?"

He held up the paper he'd been reading. A large ad in a series of pictures stretched across the page. Depicted and painstakingly numbered were (1) the morning look (brown roll-on mascara), (2) the afternoon look (blue color and black eyeliner), (3) the witching hour look (green lids), and (4) the evening look (lavender larded with silver or gold). All with matching lashes.

"So what?" I asked guardedly, watching him through narrowed (afternoon look) lids to search out any lurking sarcasm.

He clasped his forehead.

"So what? Think of the expense!" This cry clearly erupted from the depths of his Teutonic soul.

"I'll bet they get eighty cents for those tubes of paint!" and he fervently repeated his little prayer of thanksgiving.

Like Mary, I held these words in my heart, pondering. In the purse on my lap lay my own newly acquired cosmetics; a blue stick (I look best in blue) and a mechanical mascara which imparts a blue haze to the eyelashes. They cost five dollars combined. And so deftly had I applied the afternoon look that it had escaped the eagle eye of Father. At least, I think it did. Anyway I felt rather smug informing him that the eye shadow was applied over the eye, and not under it, as he had supposed.

Coming home from the hospital in the early dusk, but still wearing my afternoon look, a thought began to nag. Was this look really necessary? What look was my soul wearing at the moment? The humble look? Nope. The love of poverty look? Nope. How about the penitent look? That might be serviceable. Anyhow, I sent a little prayer skyward that it was someday going to wear the look that Christ recognized as belonging to Him. Madison Avenue hasn't worked out that one.

The Open Road

Have you gone camping yet? Do you know the smell of the pine woods at dawn, the glory of a sunrise over a sparkling little lake, with the promise of bacon and eggs just beginning to come true? You have never lived if you must answer no. Of course, you have missed a few other thrills as well, like the whir of the swamp mosquito at dusk, the drama of keeping a tent erect during a thunderstorm, and the unforgettable slog through knee-deep mud to that lake "that only the Indians know about."

Camping for us evolved out of my husband's firm conviction that Illinois, Wisconsin, and Minnesota were all lamentably fished out, no matter what the sports magazines said. The only place where fish had been saved from extinction, he said, were the remoter reaches of Canada and Alaska. My uncle DC (his real name is Dennis, but he never permitted that fact to be brunted abroad), once stated his theory on fishermen.

"People from Illinois," he mused, "always go to Wisconsin to fish; the people from Wisconsin, on the other hand, go to Minnesota, while the Minnesota fishermen go to Canada." The opening of fishing season, therefore, is the signal for great internal migrations throughout the Middle West, with each fisherman heading north from wherever he happens to live. I recently met a man from Kentucky who says he always comes to Illinois for the big ones.

My husband, however, is a big thinker. He skips over three states to his happy fishing grounds. And the lakes he has in mind are all remote, hidden in the mists of time and known only to the red men and to God. The only possible access is on foot, and camping seemed the most logical means of attaining this remote aquarium.

So we bought a tent. Not the pantywaist, umbrella kind featured at Sears, Roebuck, which could be opened with the flick of the wrist. No, ours was Army surplus, coated with creosote that was almost dry, and weighing about one hundred and fifty pounds. It had stunning accessories: long poles and ropes and little pegs to be hammered into the sod. We rented a little trailer to accommodate the big top, and in it we also stashed a stove, sleeping bags, canned goods enough to see us through the winter, and our suitcases.

We took off: Al, myself, and the three oldest children, to my mother's worried admonitions about keeping the children's feet dry, and their ears covered against drafts. She dwelt at length upon the earache theme, stating that if the children rode for three or four days in the back seat with the windows open, they would all have earaches. We nodded indulgently, and promised to be careful. Mother is such a darling—always worrying about things needlessly. We waved good-by to her and the baby, and rode off. We also were waving good-by to the washing machine, stove, comfortable beds, warm baths, and dry clothes; but we didn't think of that at the time.

The first night of camping was truly heavenly. The tent creaked protestingly, but we got it up in a little less than two hours. It had a sag in the middle, like a sway-backed horse, but it was up, by golly. Al made a fire and began to cook dinner, while the children and I fixed the sleeping bags, and unpacked the food and clothes we would need for the next morning. There was a convenient bit of civilization at the campsite, a little cluster of buildings thoughtfully provided by a beneficent government, where we could shower and buy milk. After dinner we sat around the fire slapping at mosquitoes and singing. It was lovely. After we put the children to bed, we watched the moon come up over the forest treetops. Then we, too, retired and slept soundly, at one with nature and the great outdoors. It was just as well, for it was the last sleep we would have for many a moon.

Next day we broke camp, the tent coming down a lot easier than it went up, and packed the car and trailer again. Northward, ever northward, past ever taller pines, little sparkling lakes which seemed to have attracted misguided fishermen. Al knew they were fishing in vain. We camped the second night in the Superior National Forest, where nature was truly in command. There were no cozy little outposts here—just giant trees, and giant mosquitoes. The tent erection clocked in at just under two hours, our progress greatly hampered by the mass attack of insect hordes, who had apparently not been fed in weeks. I bathed the children in DDT, which seemed a poor substitute for their usual bath, but they were game. The temperature rose to ninety-five, and we had a choice of lying on top of the sleeping bags and being eaten alive or crawling into eiderdown and roasting. We were struggling with this dilemma when the rains came.

And, in the words of the song: Lord, didn't it rain! It thundered down in white sheets of icy fury. Al and I spent the night swathed in oilskins hammering the pegs in tighter around the tent, and wondering how much longer the thing would continue to remain upright. Dawn found us like drowned rats with little appetite. We slapped the soggy tent into the trailer, wrung out the sleeping bags,

and headed for the nearest drive-in restaurant for hot coffee and breakfast.

It was late that afternoon that the earaches began. First Laurie, who was the youngest, began to complain of the pain in her ear. The next morning, as we pulled wearily along the St. Lawrence, we had three weeping children in the back seat. We spent the remainder of the trip bounding from hospital to hospital thoughout Canada. I'll say this for the Canadian hospitals. They administered relief to the poor travelers with a truly Christian courtesy. All three children were given penicillin and had their heads wrapped up like mummies. We found a little hotel in Quebec, where we bedded our poor sick family down and worried mightily about mastoids.

At the end of the week, during which neither of us slept much, the local doctor said it might be safe to try to drive home again. Poor Al never did get a line wet during the whole time. The hotel owner showed him a washtub filled with brook trout, but when my husband grabbed his rod and made for the door, he was informed that only club members could fish the lake they had come from.

On the way home I developed a stiff neck which turned me about at an interesting forty-five degree angle, and made every little pebble in the road seem like a boulder. We pulled into Oak Park sadder, but wiser. It was three or four years before we let Mother in on the fact that her little warnings had been justified.

Al goes fishing with his poker club now. To Canada.

The Job Hunt

Undoubtedly some of the finest creative writing of the day flows from the pens of ad writers, notably the ads in the Help Wanted columns. I read them regularly, and avidly, though as a homemaker with five children I needed another job as much as I needed another hole in my head.

It must be the romance of the thing that attracts me. I find a vicarious thrill picturing myself as the personal secretary to an internationally famous scientist, or the "girl Friday" (this is a widely overused term) for the rising young executive. For about fifteen minutes each morning, over coffee, I pick out the most promising positions available, mentally calculating installments on a mink stole or a trip to Bermuda, and then begin defrosting the refrigerator. This brings me down to earth fast, except yesterday morning.

Yesterday morning the following ad penetrated the winter gloom of our dining room like a tropical sunrise:

Public
Relations
Consultant.

We will train a dynamic, mature (25–50) woman for an executive position on our staff. Duties will include public relations' visits to Chicago's leading industry, and consultation with personnel directors regarding current job market trends and new developments in personnel practices. Poise, grooming, and personality extremely important. You will represent a professional staff comprised of former advertising, sales, education, accounting and personnel people who are outstanding in the counseling field. Four weeks' vacation the first year, air-conditioned central Loop office. $484.38 to start, increasing to $683.92. Please contact Miss X, X Personnel—Room 715.

There was something about this ad that attracted me. I think it was that line where the starting salary was mentioned. I'm not good at arithmetic, but even I could figure out that this was a weekly rate of about $121.00 and I knew just where I could latch onto a little domestic for about $40.00 a week. I know I'm mature (25–50) and I believe that I could be dynamic as all get out for a starting salary of $484.38 per month. I donned my black wool, drew on a pair of fresh white gloves, and sallied forth.

Miss X was the feminine version of the rising young executive: tweedy, becomingly bespectacled, and yes, dynamic. In three minutes' time she had offered me a cigarette, lit one herself, conveyed the impression that she approved of my white-gloved approach to this interview, and had a complete résumé of my previous job experience. Leaning forward in a very earnest manner, she sketched a brief, but unenlightening picture of the position in question, which she called a professional service, requiring a license to practice. Seeming to sense my mystified state of mind, she handed me a manual marked "Confidential Information" which she suggested I read, adding that any questions might be jotted down for further discussion.

The manual made it all as clear as day. This job paid

no salary. It was run on a complete commission basis—18 per cent of whatever fee the agency was able to extract from the employer, which was a fee of 72 per cent of the first month's salary of the job seeker, who was hereinafter referred to as the applicant. The first question I jotted down for further discussion was, "How has that fascinating figure of $484.38 been determined?"

Wading farther into the icy waters, I found that a training program took one month, during which time it was only a dim possibility that any commissions would be forthcoming.

There followed the most prickly set of rules since Hoyle, regarding the possibility, nay, probability of errors creeping into one's handling of the job orders, in which case Consultant B had the right to claim the commission, simply by making a claim at the proper desk, within a specified time. One might challenge another's claim, and upon submitting the proper evidence, snag the commission. I've seen enough gold mining movies to recognize this procedure; the claims office, the claim jumpers, the time limit, the whole bit. All of this, of course, suggested the possibility of friendly competition within the ranks, which led to my next question: "Were the counselors, in fact, competing with one another for the job orders and applicants?" Several other questions began to present themselves, like "What is the average salary of the present consultants," and "What do you mean, a four-week vacation? On a commission basis this simply means you're out of work for four weeks, doesn't it?"

I brought my manual and list of queries back to Miss X. She read through my questions, and allowed a look of reproach to replace the smile. Somehow she managed to convey the impression that I wasn't playing the game. I had spoiled things by being vulgar.

"You seem quite preoccupied with money, Mrs. Anton," she said at last. It was, I admitted, precisely this lure that had brought me hence. This terrible admission won an admonition that would have done a mother superior proud. The job, Miss X averred, was one of personal service to the applicants who came through those doors (we turned to look at the doors), applicants who frequently were very poor ("Do not, under any circumstances, offer them lunch money") and whose plight would haunt the dreams of the top-notch consultant. I admitted that this was a wonderful opportunity to do good, and that I was not adverse to serving mankind when I could, but that $484.38 was certainly going to be a real incentive to do a dynamic job—and to get back to my question—just how was that figure arrived at? Miss X did a couple of verbal overhead drives, during which several statements whizzed by me, one of which was something about this figure being guaranteed after the training course was completed —provided, of course, that the consultant passed the course, and obtained the license that made her a genuine unpaid professional consultant. "After all," she said, "this is a tremendous salary, and we can't hire just anyone and expect them to earn a salary like that." And she smiled invitingly, to show that I had an inside track as far as she was concerned.

Then she came to my question about just what the average salary was currently, and she once again wore the pained look. "In this office, Mrs. Anton," she said, her voice ringing with *esprit de corps*, "we do not pry into the private earnings of our consultants. Each consultant is her own boss here, working as an agent for the agency.

Her earnings are no one's business but hers." That lovely $484.38 was fading farther and farther into never-never land.

A swift glance around the office at the consultants told the story Miss X was working so hard to conceal. There were about fifteen women there, and not a dynamo in the battery. Those little tell-tale signs a woman interprets so easily were everywhere present: faces wearing the frustrations and disappointments of this "glamour job" as plainly as their tired walk and nervous handling of the phones. Clothing was worn past fashion, and no one had had a manicure or professional hair styling in years. If there was one person in that office (other than Miss X) who was managing to earn a decent salary under the system of rules, she must have been spending her afternoons at the race track. Women who are well paid invariably show it in their dress.

Miss X sensed my disenchantment. Making an appointment for several days hence, "to give you a chance to talk this over with your husband, and see whether you are willing to make this tremendous investment of time and heart in a career in this field," we parted.

My husband tied together all the loose ends on our ride home. He admitted that Miss X was probably a personnel expert with a degree to prove it. He was certain that the rest of the setup was as phony as a three-dollar bill. He'd give a lot to know what the job turnover among the consultants actually was, and he guessed that they remained at their post in this altruistic frame of mind just long enough to latch onto the first good-paying job that came through the office. It would take the average mature woman (25–50) from one month to ninety days to discover that she could not live on the meager commissions available. Still, the agency was hiring the cheapest labor in the world today, for during the time the woman did work for them she did so for practically nothing.

He may, of course, be all wrong about this. Perhaps those consultants were really earning $484.38 per month and stashing it away in the basement. I'm not going back to find out.

Dr. McEnery

Our pediatrician died a few months ago. His passing marked the end of an era for us; for he had been our partner in the building of the five healthy youngsters around us, and more than anyone else except God Himself had been our physician, adviser, and counselor in all that related to their welfare.

Having been reared during an era when Young Doctor Kildare and the irascible Doctor Gillespie personified medical perfection, I came to the business of choosing a doctor with certain preconceived notions. It seemed to me that the ideal pediatrician would be somewhere between the young man with the dream and the old man with the ulcer. My father settled it for us. He suggested Dr. Eugene McEnery, who had been a classmate at St. Ignatius, and who had been endowed by Dad with all the virtues he reserves for his old classmates. So we called Dr. McEnery and continued to do so for the next twenty years.

Dad was right. In twenty years of caring for our children, Dr. McEnery never slipped on a wrong diagnosis or failed us when we needed him. There have been anxious moments with each of the children; moments when I'd phone him with panic in my throat. Questioning me calmly, he could soothe my fears and tell me exactly what to do.

Through the formula and teething stage, the vaccinations and preschool checkups, the pre-camp era, the poi-

son-ivy-wasp-bite epoch, and down the old familiar fever-
and-rash trail of chicken pox, measles, and mumps, he was
our man. He taught me to make farina without lumps,
how to make a heat lamp for earaches, how to assign
household chores, and how to plan for college funds.

Dr. McEnery was born, reared, and educated in Chicago. Life began for him in the family home at Lytle and
Polk Streets in 1898. This house, prophetically, later became the headquarters of the Columbus Extension Hospital founded by Mother Cabrini, from which that dynamic
little saint directed and planned the hospital foundation
which is known today by her new name, St. Frances
Xavier Cabrini. John McEnery, his father, a grocer, often
supplied the saint and her sisters with groceries, and during these years, also, William Byrnes, a grain dealer,
supplied them with grain for their horses. William Byrnes'
daughter, Eleanor, was to grow up and eventually marry
John McEnery's son, Eugene. One of the McEnery family's most highly prized possessions is a relic of the saint
brought to them from Rome by Dr. Moorehead, dean of
Loyola's medical school, at the time of Mother Cabrini's
beatification.

After his high school years at St. Ignatius, Eugene Mc-
Enery entered the Navy, where he served as an ensign
during the First World War. Upon his return from service,
he entered Loyola Medical School, and upon completion
of his studies there, interned at Cook County Hospital.
During his residency at Children's Memorial Hospital, Dr.
Brenneman who was chief of staff, interested the young
doctor in empyema of the lung. For a long period of time
this condition captivated his interest, and led eventually
to his life-long work with lung disorders, particularly tuberculosis in children. Dr. McEnery was one of the few

physicians in Chicago to merit memberships in both the American College of Chest Physicians and the American Academy of Pediatrics. For twenty-five years of his professional life, he gave one morning a week to the task of examining children with TB at the Municipal Tuberculosis Sanitarium.

When Frank Lewis, the Chicago philanthropist, founded Lewis Memorial Hospital, he chose Dr. McEnery to head the pediatric department. His skillful and highly professional approach to this work quickly made the charity ward one of the finest nurseries in all of Chicago. Typically, Dr. McEnery refused any recognition of his eighteen years of service to the poor of Chicago. He preferred to look upon the experience as a priceless opportunity to examine newborns by the thousand every year, in contrast to the few hundred normally seen in pediatric practice.

For about thirty-four years, Dr. McEnery taught pediatrics at Loyola University's medical school, later called Stritch School of Medicine. My brother Tom, himself a capable and dedicated doctor, says that this course by Dr. McEnery was one of the finest he received, and also that it scared the life out of him! As a teacher, Dr. McEnery was able to pass on his practical, down-to-earth approach to medical science. His belief in his profession as a sacred trust so permeated his life and work that there was little room for meaningless tangents or the fun-and-games approach to his class. When he taught, it was with the same hard-driving energy that drove him from his bed at night to tend a sick child. "He put the fear of God in us," Tom recalls, gratefully.

That Dr. McEnery himself was God-fearing was clearly evident. The father of a large family told me of the time his five-month-old daughter lay dying. For two weeks a mounting tide of crises had been building, and when it reached its crest, Dr. McEnery told the distraught parents that only God could save her ebbing life. He told them to pray. When, at length, their prayers were answered, and the well child was restored to her mother, the parents joined the long list of those who thanked God for Dr. McEnery.

His complete giving of his gifts to sick children made him impatient with those whose attitudes were petty. Once, upon overhearing a middle-aged nurse complaining to a group of student nurses about the "crying brats getting on my nerves," he gave her a royal dressing down she would never forget. In far from gentle tones he made it clear that her unprofessional attitude not only brought her suitability as a nurse into question, but ranked her as a highly undesirable influence on the younger nurses. The nurses and sister-nurses revered him. They had witnessed his quiet, laborious hours bending over tiny cribs, and saw the special smile sick children always had from him.

When the parents came to his office with their children, it was the professional man they saw. His handling of parents was brisk. The social amenities were kept to a minimum. He reasoned, quite correctly, that his fee was primarily for advice, not conversation. Junior's new suit would be passed over without comment, but Dr. McEnery could spot a symptom in Junior's behavior which had escaped even the mother's eagle eye, and he could identify it, and tell her how to cope with it. Here, again, he was a great teacher. He never attempted to awe with his grasp of medical terminology; he spoke with convincing authority in language anyone could understand. He instructed in a no-nonsense style in the manner of a West Point drill instructor.

He refused to worship at the shrine of miracle drugs. There was something comfortingly sane in his reluctance to jump on each medical band wagon that passed by. He waited and measured results before adopting new procedures. The only time my children were administered penicillin was while we were on vacation far from home. Dr. McEnery possessed that sense that is all too uncommon, compounded of knowledge, experience, and a disciplined, balanced judgment.

There are many stories which could be related about Dr. McEnery. Every really good doctor has his precious store of infants who lived because of his genius, and adults who owe him their vigor and health. But there is little doubt that the finest proof of Dr. McEnery, both as doctor and as man, is demonstrated in the family of five sons he left behind.

The two eldest, John and Eugene, Jr., are both Chicago physicians. William is in business, Charles is a Jesuit seminarian, and Paul is a student at Stritch School of Medicine. I had the good fortune of observing the early youth of these boys, having lived across the street from them for over fourteen years.

Mrs. McEnery, a gracious and charming lady, made certain that these youngsters were given all that would make them gentlemen. Theirs was a cultured, loving home, where values were high, and where the parents were in control of the situation from the beginning. There were no "hot rods" in front of that home. I doubt whether the term "teenager" was ever recognized there. The McEnery boys were children first, and then they were young men. Today, they are men indeed.

Dr. McEnery, who used his own time for the advancement of medicine everywhere, was known throughout the state for his wisdom. Perhaps nowhere was this quality more easily seen than in his role as parent and husband. People who had no occasion to request his professional services could, by casual observance of the father, form an accurate image of the pediatrician. The time he had to give his family was necessarily limited. It was carefully hoarded between the hours of his professional life, but he turned it into a treasure for them. When they were little, he took his boys tobogganing, they attended Burton Holmes films, and whenever the circus was in town, he saw to it that they went together. Later on, the boys were included in more grown-up activities, but these, too, were of a nature that would instruct and elevate their growing intellects rather than just amuse. Their allowances were just enough to supply the normal needs of their age. As soon as they were old enough, each of them worked summers and part-time around the neighborhood to earn extra money for whatever they wished. This savings program enabled most of them to see much of America and Europe.

Dr. and Mrs. McEnery loved to travel, and they saw much of the world after the children were older. But minor frivolities, such as movies, were passed over in favor of the company of friends. Doctor loved music; particularly the type of music made by happy people around a piano. A television drama existed outside his realm of thought; a few bars of music played in a living room drew him like a magnet. He remained remarkably untouched by the spectator culture of our age. He was a worker with a higher purpose. That this work often brought little monetary reward was unworthy of his consideration. Healing was his life, and healing was his deft, sure touch.

Dr. McEnery can never be replaced. It is to be hoped that the three physicians he leaves behind will inspire the admiration and confidence their father earned. For he did far more for his patients than devise formulas and vaccinate. He set for all of us a living example of how to be a parent.

Not long ago, his widow was presented with a testimonial from the Tuberculosis Institute of Chicago and Cook County. It reads as follows:

WHEREAS, the kindly Providence that endowed Dr. Eugene T. McEnery with his many virtues has called him to a higher sphere, and

WHEREAS, The Tuberculosis Institute of Chicago and Cook County by his death has lost an associate whose life was devoted in full measure to the service of humanity, now

THEREFORE BE IT RESOLVED, that the Board of Directors of the Tuberculosis Institute of which he was a valued member for ten years, places in its records a testimonial of his contributions to the welfare of his community, noting especially his concern for children and the unfortunate, and expressing to his family and his friends the consolation that he will be remembered as one who truly let his light shine before men.

Adopted at Chicago, Illinois
September 12, 1962

Grant Park

Music and scenic settings have long been mated for the pleasures of sight and sound. Interlochen, in Michigan, has proven the soundness of the combination for musical scholarship as well. The Germans and Swiss have, for centuries, floated music in the open air of a natural setting, and when I was a child, the little Sunday evening band concerts in the Chicago parks were a source of delight and mosquito bites in equal portions. It was natural for the park district to place a giant shell in the middle of Grant Park, and produce a program of music for Chicagoans that was free to all who would come. The mosquitoes are still around, to some degree, but more pestiferous are the little monoplanes taking off and landing at Meigs Field across the drive. In spite of them, however, the Grant Park concerts attract thousands of music lovers every night of the season. They come in droves to sit on the benches and listen, or lie on the grass and picnic to music.

One evening, when Jan Peerce was there, I took my eldest, Ann, to hear the great tenor sing. Next to us on the bench was a middle-aged couple who knew all about him. They told us, while the orchestra tuned up, about his background and early days of struggle. Then he sang, and the night was breathless, catching the golden notes. A path of moonlight lay quiet in the musing lake, mirroring the magic of his song. When it ended, thousands of hands beat their wild approval, and my male informant nudged me blissfully,

"Isn't he fat? Boy! Is that Jan Peerce fat!" And with that he returned to the task of clapping vigorously for an encore. It left me pondering. A status symbol, perhaps? Was being fat the greatest thing he could say about the tenor? I'm still uncertain. This kind of conversation flourishes in Chicago.

A short walk north from the shell brings the casual stroller within the sound of splashing waters, and the impressive fountain Kate Buckingham bequeathed to the city of Chicago. If one is fortunate enough to strike it properly, the colored lights will be illuminating the sparkling show, chromatically shifting through a rainbow of splendor. The fountain shoots higher at these times, and on hot evenings the spray falls hundreds of feet from the fountain in beneficent mist upon the little congress of tourists and Chicagoans who gather there after the concert.

When Queen Elizabeth and Prince Philip visited Chicago in July of 1959, the full power of Buckingham Fountain was brought to bear upon what was one of the loveliest sights I have ever seen: the ceremonies and formal departure of the royal couple. The British yacht *Britannia* was anchored off the Buckingham Plaza, about a quarter-mile into the lake, looking like a great birthday cake, many-tiered, and twinkling with candles. The night was a blissfully cool seventy degrees, and my husband and I were lying on our stomachs on the roof of a tugboat near the *Britannia*, viewing a scene that was unforgettable.

The sky was dark blue, and the Chicago skyline alight in familiar beauty. The fountain, a volcano of color and splendor, formed the backdrop for a red-carpeted plaza where the city officials bade farewell to Elizabeth and Philip and their party, who then boarded launches and

crossed the span to their yacht while the city fireboats
erupted with water pyrotechnics, and a fireworks bouquet
sent golden flowers across the velvet sky. The Queen of
England saluted all the little boats that had drawn close
to say good-by, and when her launch finally reached the
Britannia, the royal visitors boarded, and we had a final
glimpse of her white handkerchief waving, before the
great yacht got slowly under way.

Soldier Field, south of the shell and of the Museum of
Natural History, is Chicago's arena where contests of
every kind, from boxing to singing, are held. Its colos-
seumed structure is ideally situated for metropolitan Chicago; the hard benches have held millions of spectators
for Army-Navy games, circuses, high school football,
police shows, and mass meetings of every kind. The
twenty-eighth Eucharistic Congress was held here, when
we were very young, and my brother Tom, returning with
the family by streetcar, sang "Cardinal Mundelein" to a
singsong of his own creation all the way home. The only
visible portion of our spiritual leader had been his little
red hat, but this had been assiduously pointed out to Tom,
and left an indelible impression.

For Chicago Catholics, the most memorable evening
spent in Soldier Field was the Marian Year Mass in 1954,
when Cardinal Stritch celebrated a Pontifical High Mass
in honor of the Blessed Mother, and a glorious full moon,
like a host in the sky, shone down on the worshiping thousands in gentle benediction. That evening, two hundred
thousand Chicago Catholics came to pay tribute to the
Mother of God. It was the largest crowd in the history
of Soldier Field.

Daisy Afternoons

Most of the nation's work is done in the morning. The cool, pre-noon hours, obligingly elastic, stretch to fit Trappist mornings (two till twelve), bankers' mornings (nine till twelve), or housewives' mornings which begin about two minutes after the baby starts crying. Alert and adaptable, motivated morning has its sleeves rolled up.

Evenings are for organized joy. Evenings may sparkle, sing or smoulder, or just sit quietly before the fire with a good book. Evenings gently harvest a whole day.

Afternoons are bonus hours. For the past thirty years, afternoons in the temperate zone have been silently building up moments of leisure time. In most households, after the lunch dishes are cleared away, there is a three or four hour oasis of repose before dinner must be cooked. Some women go bowling, or shopping, or hike through a wood. Some play bridge or attend lengthy luncheon meetings. Some escape to golf courses, or cocktail parties. Some roll their hair on curlers and give themselves facials. Some, like me, for instance, enjoy an afternoon at the Art Institute or shopping in the Loop.

Our museum of art has two bronze lions guarding its doorway. Inside is a fine collection of French Impressionists, an oriental exhibit, a fabulous housing of porcelain and glasswares, treasures of Old Masters, antique furnishing, the world-famed Thorne rooms in miniature, and a horrendous clutter of modern art.

Within well-defined limits, modern art, it seems to

me, can do a colorful and pleasant service. It is no mean
thing to enhance the shelves of a supermarket with good
design and cherry color. A well-packaged slab of frozen
peas has its place in the scheme of things. What gives me
pause, and creates small nagging fears about taste in
general, is the sight of these wildly inept daubs of paint
skewered onto canvas and hanging on the walls of a famous art gallery. Nevertheless, these prehensile produc-
tions are there. Obviously one must cope in some fashion:
a few rules might be useful.

Rule 1. Never begin your tour with the Old Masters.
This scheme will find you at the end of the afternoon
among the moderns, with a splitting headache, a desire to
kick small children, and a disoriented psyche. Upon entering the gallery, go at once to the modern art exhibit. Take
a quick gander at the latest conversation pieces, taking
notes, if possible. This will provide interesting discussion
material at the next book club meeting. Then, turning
your face against the tide, enjoy a stroll backward in time.

Gaze at Gauguin; laugh with Renoir; revel in Corot;
and slowly, as the flaming Turners and the spacious, gracious landscapes of Gainsborough light up the corners of
your soul, re-enter the beauty of the past. Telescoped and
condensed into jewels, these paintings of long ago quiver
with elemental fire. Wander through the Dutch schools
and listen to the song of domestic harmony they sing.
Find winding through the Renaissance and before it the
great spiritual heritage of the West: the compassionate
Christ leaning from His mother's knee, or hanging from
His cross. Leave the museum only after one more long
look at a masterpiece like the "Assumption" of El Greco,
and you will return to your own world a whole person,

richer in understanding and refreshed for having immersed an afternoon in the well of the past.

Rule 2. Practice self-restraint while viewing modern art. There are few such fertile spots for this discipline. It took years to accomplish, but I recently walked through an entire modern art collection without turning a hair. This kind of restraint is rarely achieved, however. I noticed one woman there helplessly leaning against a wall in the throes of a hysterical convulsion. She was viewing, through widespread fingers, a wall piece resembling a junkyard in which all the car parts had been welded together and enameled. It looked like a rather nasty accident. An elderly gentleman, his legs apart and his arms akimbo, repeated loud ejaculations while staring at a prize-winning painting which consisted of a yellow stripe wittily superimposed on a black background the size of a grandstand. I shall omit discussion of a tight little cordon of youth whose rejection was expressed in more graphic terms.

Reaction is bound to come. Modern art, unfortunately, thrives on it. It takes the "I don't care what they say about it, as long as they talk about it" approach. The only possible response to modern art is a tight-lipped stoicism. The slightest facial twitch may be seized upon as a comment. Laugh or cry only in the privacy of your own home.

Rule 3. Resist the temptation to rehang these modern canvases to suit yourself. These highly colored escapades may be more agreeable seen from another angle, but the museum guards tend to be stuffy about rearrangements. I have suspected, however, that this is precisely what the guards do in their off-hours. This year's showing looks so familiar that I have a feeling I saw some of those hand-knit bronzes last year, only right side up. And I distinctly remember that vast yellow stripe! It was out by the stair-way last year, on its side. Someone has cunningly removed the arrow and the "exit" sign.

Rule 4. Shield the children, at all costs. Take them through the pottery exhibit, visit the Thorne rooms, visit the museum store. Buy them replicas of Aztec jewelry if you can't settle for ice cream later, but don't take them near the modern art. Inevitably they will giggle loud enough to injure the sensitive beatniks worshiping there, or boast that they could draw better than that in second grade. In any case, it will prove an unnerving experience for all concerned, and may cripple their attitude toward all art. Barbie, who is eleven, having been exposed to a unique creation compounded of glue, sand, ants, axle grease and mustard, wanted to know "How did this junk get into the art show, Mother?" at the top of her lungs, and left me at a loss for words.

Barbara's Sunday afternoons have taken on a quality of fact-finding that makes me realize that none of the past is ever really lost. Life brings back to all of us the things that were before. In ever-widening concentric circles, the past, present, and future meld and mingle; the more things are different, the more they are the same. Recently Barbara and I set out together to explore the Oriental Institute.

Founded by James H. Breasted in 1919, with the aid of a large subsidy from John D. Rockefeller, the Oriental Institute is a splendid ornament to the University of Chicago campus. We found within its walls an impressive array of artifacts from the Institute's own expeditions to Egypt and the Near East. Barb was able to see papyrus, mummies, model pyramids, cuneiform writings, shards and bowls dating from five thousand years ago. There was a veritable treasure of golden ornaments and jewelry found in the tombs and under the floor stones of the homes of ancient princes.

A winged bull from Assyria, a gigantic statue of King Tutankhamen, twin bull columns, god gate pieces from Sargon's palace, wall pieces and friezes taken from the tombs—we were immersed in the depths of an archaeological treasure trove. We found a model of the column on which was inscribed the Code of Hammurabi. I had thought it would have been on a scroll or something, but there it was, hammered out of stone, in precise cuneiform writing, neatly covering the entire four sides of the column, and measuring about ten feet in height.

Of greatest interest to Barb was the Egyptian exhibit. Breasted, a noted archaeologist, had been instrumental in the discovery of King Tutankhamen's tomb. The Oriental Institute has an impressive collection of mummies in ornamented cases, and these were the object of Barb's tour. She wanted to see what they looked like, and she was thoroughly shocked and thrilled. The blackened remains of an elderly lady, from which the wrappings about the head had been removed, will remain in her imagination for a long time. We turned from this to examine a model of a temple and pyramid, but I could see her large hazel eyes still glancing over her shoulder at the grisly sight. I imagine the sixth grade heard all about it.

We finally left and wandered into the Rockefeller Memorial Chapel, which is large, Gothic, gray, and cold. Barb was intrigued by the velvet padded seats for the congregation, and when she discovered there were no kneelers, she asked about it. I told her the people who worship here either stand or sit during the services. She thinks they are lucky.

We concluded the afternoon with a luncheon at Morton House, on the lake front. Barb had a lovely time ordering her luncheon from the waitress all by herself. As we ate, she chatted about our excursion, and shivered with delighted horror over the mummy.

In about five years, I thought, Billy will be ready for this trip; after that, perhaps the grandchildren. Al and I will come back to the Oriental Institute, just the two of us; though it seems a waste not to have a child along. Through young eyes we see so much more; pulled along by their enthusiasm and keen sense of discovery, we more truly explore and learn. It is likely that my father discovered this long ago.

I prefer afternoons for shopping. Through long and painful experience, I have finally discovered that the only way to shop successfully is to leave the children at home. Unless they themselves are the target for the purchases, children tend to distract from the purpose of trips to the store. They're always wanting to stop for hamburgers when I'm tracking down outsized curtains, or slipping into the French Room to try on the hats amid giggles (their own) and glares (the saleswomen's). I leave them home and take the El into the Loop.

People one meets in Chicago's Loop are frequently not native Chicagoans. They are here on convention from Galesburg, or Moline, and have promised to bring something back for Aunt Helen from Marshall Field's. Or they live in Wisconsin, and are in Chicago to visit the oculist.

Every corner is curdled with sailors from Great Lakes. And for the most part, the crowds are detached, hurried, and wearing that harassed look occasioned by the knowledge that the store is closing in five minutes and they haven't finished shopping yet.

Some of them are elderly ladies who enter the mainstream of life again when they go to the Loop. You see them in the dining rooms of the stores, sipping tea and watching style shows. One of these took an active interest in my search for a winter coat the other day. She was sitting on a comfortable green couch in the coat department, and I thought she was waiting for someone. It developed that her purchase had been completed an hour before, but she was fascinated by the spectacle of women trying on one coat after another and viewing themselves in the mirror. She eyed me with friendly interest, and after I had doffed the third coat, she spoke up:

"Try that blue one, dear. It should go well with your eyes." I had planned to try it anyway, so I did. But she didn't like the way it hung in the back.

"No dear, take it off—it's all wrong for you—way too much fullness there." And she went over to the rack and selected a black one, with a little mink collar.

"That's more like it, dear. Do you own a black coat now?" I admitted that I did not, whereupon she insisted that I buy black, because every wardrobe, she felt, needed a good basic black coat. After that, she agreed, I would be able to buy a colored one.

The price of the coat she selected was too high, however, so I finally bought a simple black coat without the fur trim. She was very pleased. She gathered up her parcels and thanked me for a lovely afternoon and headed for the elevator.

But our afternoons are not always so peaceful. Usually afternoons at home are climaxed by Al's return from the office. When the children were very young, there was a ritual of preparation for this highlight of the day. It involved baths all around, fresh dresses and shirts, hair ribbons and admonitions to "stay clean until Daddy comes home." There were occasions, however, when plans, in the best tradition of mice and men, went haywire.

Like the time Al came up the driveway one late summer afternoon and saw Sarge up on the garage roof with his bicycle. Al struggled to keep his voice even.

"Sarge," he called, as quietly as possible, so as not to

frighten him, "what are you doing up there?" Sarge made what was for him a completely logical explanation.

"Well, I got on this roof, see, and I thought to myself, I wonder if I can get my bike up here too. So I got this rope and tied it around the bike, and I hauled it up here all by myself."

Al took a firmer hold of his temper, and said, through noticeably clenched teeth:

"Come down off the roof, Sarge. Leave the bike where it is, and just come down." And then he went off into the house in search of a soothing glass of milk. It was some hours before he trusted himself to go into the matter further. By this time, of course, Sarge had forgotten all about the incident, and wondered what Daddy was upset about.

One sunny afternoon in June as I was preparing to leave for my weekly raid on the grocery store, Al volunteered to direct my precarious maneuvering of the car backward down the driveway. He stood protectingly against the shrubbery along the drive, wigwagging his arms and clutching his forehead in mock despair. As I drew abreast of him, he flattened himself against the bushes, and the car neatly pinned him in place. I chose to stop at that point rather than remove his shirt buttons, and he began a lengthy dissertation on my driving. Pinned as he was, he could move neither right nor left, and it was here that Laurie, who was standing on the side porch watching the proceedings with keen interest while absently fiddling with the handle of the sprinkling system, inadvertently flipped it to the "on" position. Al, unfortunately, was standing directly over one of the nozzles, which emitted a pretty spray of water all about him, like a fountain.

His first shocked gasp alerted Laurie, who froze in horror while our captive chief did a water ballet punctuated by maddened shouts. When she came to, it was to turn and flee indoors. I finally recovered myself enough to move the car slowly away from the aquacade so he could escape. He sloshed up the stairs after Laurie, but was so bogged down by his waterlogged condition that by the time he found her he could see the humor of the situation.

Laurie has always been fleet. Our first daughter, Ann, was the kind of child who enjoyed dolls, tea parties, Girl Scouting, and all the feminine little things associated with being a feminine little thing. Our second daughter, Laurie, had beautiful big blue eyes, a satin complexion, a lovely smile, and a desire to corner the world market on toy guns. We bought her dolls each Christmas—they were still like new the following Christmas. She simply never went near them. What she wanted, it developed, was a train, some trucks, a fort, a lantern for the fort, and another gun and holster.

I recall the Easter when I went all out to get her the most beautiful Easter outfit obtainable: a ruffled dress, a princess coat, a flower-trimmed bonnet, little white gloves, and new patent leather slippers. Early Easter morning she arose and dressed in her finery, and tiptoed into our room to whisper in my ear:

"I'm going to go to an early Mass, Mother, so I can come home and play cowboys with Kit." I opened one eye and took in the resplendent pink figure, but found something oddly amiss. There was a large bulge around the waist of the fitted coat.

"What's wrong with your coat, Laurie? There's a funny bulge at the waist," I said, reaching out to examine it.

Laurie turned and swiftly made for the door.

"I'm wearing my gun and holster, Mother, so I'll be ready to play when I get back home. No one will ever notice it under my coat."

It's not the easiest thing in the world to pursue an agile child down the stairs at five in the morning, but I made it.

Keeping the Records Straight

The next time one of those bright-eyed statisticians ropes off a little area for investigation, called, for example, "How The American Housewife Spends Her Day," and fences it with an impenetrable barbed wire of figures and graphs, I'd like him (it's always a *him*) to do me one small favor. I'd like him to include somewhere between the dark and the daylight a large patch of wasted time devoted to the care and maintenance of hifi records! These sleuths invariably remember all the useless trips to the pantry (dotted lines tracing and retracing one another), but leave out all the chores wished on us by the Great American Male who insists on inventing things to raise our standard of living. Woman in America today now finds herself at such a high level of existence that she can only survive in that rarified atmosphere by perfecting the skills of plumbing, electronics, decorating, carpentry, bricklaying, gardening, and the delicate manipulation necessary to replace the disposable bags in her vacuum cleaner. To hire a repairman for her collection of gadgets would be so expensive that she would have to drop several brackets in living standards in order to pay him. Enterprising Do It Yourself advertisers were the first to grasp this truth. These ads always show a fragile, feminine person Doing It Herself. The advent of hifi has brought in its wake a whole new dimension of time consumption which is, of course, the responsibility of the housewife.

Back in the olden times when we were first married, my

husband and I were given a phonograph and we began to collect records. Zealous for the musical culture of yet unborn children, we laid in a supply of records—symphonies, concertos, operas—and larded it generously with our particular favorites of the concert stage. John Charles Thomas, John McCormack, Gladys Swarthout, Lily Pons, Jussi Bjoerling, Beniamino Gigli, as well as Yehudi Menuhin, Alexander Brailowsky, Ignace Paderewski, and so on. In all those years of caring for these musical children, I can recall no sleepless nights. They rested quietly in their grooves, until called to life by the needle, which was replaced once or twice a year at a cost of about fifty cents. They were breakable records, so I kept them high up on a shelf where they would be safe from the onslaught of a growing family.

Purchasing these records had an old-fashioned quaintness about it. My husband and I would leisurely wander into a record shop and before you could say "impulse buying," were deep in the catalogue of classical records searching for titles we felt would enrich our lives. Armed with a large stack of records, we would retire into a cubicle fitted with a phonograph and play each of these potential purchases, criticize them with all the insouciance of Paul Hume, and then buy one record which was clearly the pick of the lot, for the price of one dollar. We would feel dangerously extravagant, and joke nervously about how we were going to make it up out of the budget. How I sigh for those tender, bygone days. (And, incidentally, that brave little budget.)

Inevitably, the higher standard of living caught up with us, and in a modest way we did our best to hold up our end of things. We bought a hifi—table model, not to be ostentatious—and embarked on a sea of unknown peril.

One of the first intimations of the albatross around our necks was the realization that we must have a *diamond* needle. The only diamond in the house heretofore was the diamond on my finger, which I guarded with my life. The diamond needle didn't look like much, but the salesman assured us that this was indeed a genuine diamond, and backed up the statement by letting us peer at it through a magnifying glass. It was sold to us bedded down on blue velvet, in a little plastic case, and it cost thirty dollars. We tried not to think about it too much, but we secretly soothed ourselves with the thought that now at last we had everything.

Then we cautiously approached the continent of hifi recordom which was still mostly untracked wilderness. I bought *Laudate Dominum,* sung by the Trappists at Gethsemane, because Thomas Merton's voice was on it; my husband bought something from Dixieland. Then (some months later) I bought two more records of a standard nature, which cost four times what our early treasures had cost, and these were my last purchases.

But in spite of my preference for college educations over hifi records, we find ourselves the owners and caretakers of some fifty-seven records at the present time. Approximately ten of these were gifts from friends at Christmas, and at least four of them, of Broadway hit shows, are the residue of the annual visits of a priest friend of ours, who, in spite of an incurable tone deafness, loves to hear *My Fair Lady, The Music Man, Destry Rides Again* and *Most Happy Fella,* in that order, played over and over during the entire week of his stay with us. The remaining records are here because of that particular combination of sheer brass and cunning which has made American big business one of the wonders of the world.

They began rolling in when my fourteen-year-old daughter succumbed to Record Club Plan advertising. Club is hardly the word—bludgeon is more like it!

Having attained the affluence that only a baby-sitter can enjoy, Ann naturally needed an outlet for her money. Deftly side-stepping the lure of the Christmas Savings Club, the Cashmere-of-the-Month Club, and the dues of that little confraternity which meets regularly at the soda fountain, she joined the Record Club Plan. It was deceptively simple. All she had to do was fill out a form, and they sent her in return three records free.

This was some time ago. Since then, our collection seems to have grown of its own accord. Like the bewitched broom carrying pails of water in Hollywood's version of *The Sorcerer's Apprentice* (starring, I believe, Mickey Mouse), these records roll into our home regularly. Every once in awhile (at no foreseeable interval) comes a little notice from the Club stating that they are poised to send her another record (at $3.98) *unless she remembers to send them the enclosed card* (Do Not Bend) begging them to desist. Naturally, human nature being what it is, this proves to be a pretty sound way of unloading records. Ann has found that her baby-sitting money, followed by her allowance and birthday money are just about enough to take care of this expense. When the third rendition of *Li'l Abner* arrived—this time the orchestrated version—I decided to take a hand in the matter. I promised Ann I'd be on the watch for these deadly missives and whip them back to the company with staggering accuracy. But the sneaky things looked so much like the advertising material that I always throw unopened into the wastebasket that this method has seldom worked either. The score so far: them, 39 records sold; us, nothing. Ann has now decided to sever connections with this enterprising concern, but if I know my daughter, she will finally get to it about four records from now—and one of them will be *Li'l Abner,* the movie sound track.

The fact remains . . . there are now these records to care for. Our marriage has also produced fifty (count 'em), fifty little fingers: the smaller ones sticky with peanut butter and jelly, and the larger ones with chewing gum, glue, axle grease, ink and waving lotion. Familiarity, they say, breeds contempt, and I can think of no other word to describe the attitude of my brood to these costly, scratchable, grease-abhoring, diamond-demanding records. I now spend, (and this is what that statistician should know) hours every week wiping from these sensitive surfaces the week's accumulation of gummy fingermarks that mar the pristine clarity of their tone. I can, of course, do nothing about the gouges; the scratches have become part of the score. You have never really heard the Velvet Fog until you have heard him gurgling through a layer of peanut butter.

And you have never seen agony until you have seen my brother-in-law listening to our records. Enshrined within his home is a magnificent Magnavox, from whose custom-fitted depths are emitted only those golden-throated tones of the highest fidelity. The needle of this instrument, diamond or no, is scrapped regularly for a new one. The control panel necessary to its operation looks like the one on a Boeing 707. The records are treated with great honor and solemnity, and their care involves all sorts of equipment: chamois, mink brushes . . . the works. Privately I have thought that this is a great deal of fuss to expend on jazz; but every man to his own poison. Someday I'd like to take his picture as he records on that mobile, sensitive face each gravelly, craggy passage—every gorge and fjord which impedes the path of music as it flows from our hifi. He usually ends the sessions by pleading, through pale and trembling lips, that we turn off the set.

Once, in a desperate attempt to inject some sort of order into the keeping of that record collection, I did invest in a tiny mink brush which was supposed to clear away those infinitesimal specks of dust that hifi can magnify into mountains. It soon became apparent that what was needed was not a brush but a scraper. Now I fill a pan with lukewarm water and a mild soap suds and firmly wash these platters as I would the dishes. Someday, if this collection gets big enough, I'm going to put the whole batch in the dishwasher. This may even remove the mastic from the tiling project which mysteriously gathered on the surface of one of them!

Washing records is only one of the time-wasters. The other one concerns filing. For each record comes in its own special cardboard case, and for sanity's sake must be replaced therein. The younger children in our family, as yet illiterate, select them purely by the pictures on the covers. The older children have a habit of extracting twenty records, placing them on the turntable, moving the volume to the highest possible decibel and then leaving the premises. I can choose between putting the records away myself, or leaving them to the mercy of the baby, who loves rolling them across the carpet. This activity can account for twenty minutes a day all by itself.

I view the sophistry of stereophonic sound with a jaundiced eye. Does anyone know where I can get an old wind-up victrola? I have some old John McCormack records I'd like to weep over some evening.

Radio

One of the surest signs of approaching age is the gradually lowered tolerance to radio. There is an ever-shortening span of enjoyment before one reaches to turn it off. My children, on the other hand, have an amazing resistance to a critical estimate of the sounds issuing forth on the airwaves, and have been known to walk about for hours with transistors glued to their ears. The fact that they can carry on normal activities and conversation meantime indicates—to me, at least—a possible addiction to a listening habit, rather than actual enjoyment.

The singing commercial has taken possession of the children. When called upon to sing, the sandbox set invariably raises its clear, childish treble in praise of a cereal or cleaning agent. Not long ago we met a Spanish doctor and his family traveling to New York. We had a pleasant journey together, and were surprised to learn that the two children spoke only Spanish. We asked the mother if the little girl would sing us a song. The mother spoke to the child in Spanish, and the little girl politely faced us and sang, in a lilting, sweet voice, a Spanish song. When she was finished, we applauded, and turned to her mother to inquire what the song was named.

"That is a little song she learned at home in Puerto Rico," said the mother, smiling. "It is about Texaco oil and gasoline."

Radio, during its golden age, was a wonderful source of pleasure. One would never dream of creating distrac-

tions during those superb programs of yore. My Grand-
father Kenter had sacred times before the old sixteen-
tuber which would have meant death to interrupt. We
tiptoed about during "Amos and Andy," silently fled
during the concert programs, and leaned forward with
breathless joy while we followed Fred Allen through
"Allen's Alley." If the streets of the neighborhood seemed
strangely quiet after four each afternoon, the initiate
knew that it was because every child on the West Side of
Chicago was lying on a living-room rug soaking up "Little
Orphan Annie," "The Secret Three," "Jack Armstrong,
All American Boy," "Sergeant Preston of the Yukon,"
"The Cisco Kid," and one or two other fifteen-minute
thrillers whose names have left me.

Fiddling with the dial of our radio, at the age of eleven
or twelve, I frequently came across a trio of singers billed
as "Al, Vic, and Will," who yodeled catchy songs compounded of intricate and complicated chord structures. I
always dialed on past them to find "Little Orphan Annie,"
in unwitting disloyalty to my future husband and his two
brothers. But this was the era of the serial program, spon-
sored by cereal. We were exhorted to inhale mountains of
breakfast food during the intermissions, while Jack Armstrong or some other hero languished in a cave of bears,
or hung perilously at the edge of a volcano. One enthusiastic announcer got us to melt butter (at forty cents a
pound) and pour it over our cereal for a "yummy treat"
while listening to the serial. We put on about fifteen
pounds apiece that winter.

Evenings of that era sparkled with golden moments
spaced throughout the week; moments dedicated to Fib-
ber McGee and Molly, Jack Benny, Burns and Allen, Joe
Penner, and Bob Hope. Comedy writing enjoyed a hey-

day; the great depression era was "mercifully tickled into saving laughter by these inspired clowns."

Growing up meant switching from Annie Rooney to James Melton. By the time I was sixteen, and at Our Lady of Angels Academy, Clinton, Iowa, I was listening to the "Firestone Hour" each week, with its matchless programs of wonderful concerts; Bishop Fulton Sheen each Sunday afternoon (the nuns' idea, actually, though we grew to love him); Easy Aces; and occasionally, the Saturday opera from the Metropolitan in New York. Music and wit were spooned out in easy doses, but no one talked during the programs. Today, there seems to be little difficulty about listening while conversing.

Recently, my daughter Ann, working as receptionist for my brother Tom, looked up to find a sweet-faced old lady entering the doctor's offices. She tottered over to the desk, and Ann noticed she was wearing a hearing aid, so she raised her voice and spoke distinctly.

"Do you wish to see Dr. Kenter?" The little old lady seemed not to hear, so Ann leaned over the desk and articulated:

"Dr. Kenter is busy at the moment, but if you'll be be seated, he'll see you very soon." The bemused face broke into a smile.

"Just a second, dearie, it's the last of the ninth, and Mickey Mantle is up next." And she pulled the transistor from her purse and turned it up so as not to miss the excitement.

I admire this devotion to sports, but I am not cut out for modern radio. I have yet to hear anything on the AM frequency that would induce me to plug it into my head and walk about with it. FM, of course, is something else again.

A friend of ours, a naval officer, advances the theory that the whole idea of "music while you work" was born in the laundry rooms of the Navy. The rooms became vestibules on Hades, he says, with the heat, steam, and profanity of about seven hundred sailors, all trying to get their laundry. Into this inferno walked an officer new to the base; he was so shocked he determined to do something to relieve conditions. He installed music over a loud-speaker system, and by the simple process of turning it up to deafening proportions, turned the atmosphere of the laundry pit from the Black Hole of Calcutta to the Merry Garden Ballroom. Our informant claims that no one from that time on got the correct laundry, simply because the guys behind the counter were inept at lip reading, but on the whole it made the experience more bearable. Anyway, to this unsung hero of the navy we owe the fact that wherever pain or discomfort is to be endured: the dentist office, the hospital, the credit bureau, the offices where men slave all day long, the beauty shops and stores where the little woman makes contact with society at large, all are flooded with music, or Muzak, as the case may be.

It seems portentous (and a thing of state) that Henrici's Restaurant, a fine eating palace in the Loop district of Chicago, and one which advertised "no orchestral din" on its menus, is at present being torn down. They made marvelous oatmeal there. Their coffee and whipped cream was a thing of beauty. And it was silent. The silver clatter and gentle clink of glassware had a way of floating into the old oil paintings on the walls and disappearing. Conversation was low and muffled. An atmosphere of almost holy quiet pervaded the soul and settled the mind. We could enter after the theater and discuss the play successfully; no one had to strain to hear. We could tiptoe in on

Sunday mornings after Mass and breakfast to the crinkle of the newspaper. No violins or saxophones. And they're tearing it down!

A passion for noise has taken possession of us all. The newest homes are being built with hifi right in the walls. The other day while shopping, I came across the ultimate. "Amuse your friends with music while you're away from the phone," read the little card on it. "It" is a little gadget on which to rest the receiver of your telephone while you go to look for something, or answer the doorbell. When in contact with the receiver, it cunningly emits little Strauss waltzes into the waiting earphone!

Noel, Noel

Christmas! The very name holds its own special magic. Christmas is white snow falling softly after midnight Mass; red-cassocked choir boys caroling lovely old hymns. Christmas is smothered laughter and whispered messages about hiding toys; it is two tired parents arranging toys underneath a tree, wearily climbing the stairs to bed at 3 A.M., knowing full well they will be awakened at 4:30 A.M., by children's shouts to come down and see what Santa brought! Christmas is eagerly waiting for the mailman and the bundle of messages from old friends; it is trying to decide where to display the Christmas cards. It means red housecoats for the girls, and red corduroy shirts for the boys, and a bustle in the kitchen early in the morning over the turkey preparation. Christmas is a constant stream of guests who drop in for a moment to exclaim over the tree and munch fruit cake. It is the flutter and tinsel of the Christmas Ball, the pretty bows and wrappings on packages, and the vain search for the box of bulbs for the tree lights. Christmas is merriment, music, and love. Christmas is the favorite time of year in any home.

When we were little, Mother and Dad began by pretending that Santa brought the tree, lights and all. Later, when midnight tree decorating became difficult to manage with wide-awake youngsters lying in bed listening for sleighbells, they informed us that they were going to help Santa's Brownies by trimming the tree themselves. This

sounded pretty logical to us, and we gladly pitched in to help. Sometimes we popped corn and strung it on the tree along with candy canes and fragile ornaments and lights. Whenever there was anyone in kindergarten or first grade, which was frequently, we had miles of colored chains laboriously manufactured with construction paper and library paste. I recall one Christmas when three or four of us had mumps and had to stay in bed. Mother moved our beds into the living room so we could enjoy the tree and the toys in perfect comfort.

Presents in those post-depression days were always of a practical nature, except for the huge box of toys sent us by Grandma Kenter. There were always toys for each of us, and new dresses or suits. One Christmas Grandpa made us a large doll house, complete with electric lights. It was big enough to play in, and there were chairs and a table inside. This toy was kept at their house. It was a great attraction for years. I also remember zeppelins, which were huge gray balloons with little cardboard carriers underneath them.

Christmas in Al's childhood was a rather different kind of affair, from his recollection of it. Santa arrived and spanked everyone. Al always dreaded the day because, as the youngest, he was certain to be given special attention by the muscular uncle who played Santa, and he was whipped soundly before being handed his present.

Our Christmas starts with Mass. Al sings the midnight Mass, and so does Ann, but in different churches. I compromise by going to hear first one and then the other, in alternate years. Barb has to sing with the children at the nine o'clock children's Mass, and Al goes back to sing the noon Mass as well. Sarge, Laurie, and I fit ourselves into this schedule somehow, but throughout the entire morning there is a constant stream of people either leaving for or returning from Mass.

Al and I have always gone all out for Christmas with our children. We used to love shopping for toys. One of the reasons why Christmas has taken on the aspect of a

giant bazaar is, I suspect, that adults are so enthralled
by the toys. Frequently the ones who enjoy the toys best
are the aunts and grandmothers. The children are momen-
tarily interested, but after the initial exploration has
passed, they are off to examine the loot of their friends.
On quiet Christmas afternoons, it is often the mother of
the family who is gently arranging the tiny furniture in
the doll house, or dressing the baby doll. It is the father,
not the son, who is switching trains and trying out the
new Erector Set.

Christmas at midday means dinner at Mother and
Dad's, with their twenty-seven grandchildren (twenty-
four of them aged twelve or younger) running around
wildly. Mother's feast is a lovely sight to behold! She
sets the long dining-room table to capacity. It extends
into the living room. The TV room is converted to a children's dining room. They are fed first so they will be finished before we sit down. The menu leans heavily on a
truly magnificent turkey, with bread stuffing and surrounded by a veritable ecumenical gathering of vegetables. Salads, spiced apples, peaches, pickles, olives, celery,
and radishes round out the side dishes, while on the buffet
rests the pies—every kind—the cakes—fluffy or fruit filled—
and the coffee. The talk is confused and constant. No one
ever really listens. Everyone just keeps talking and laugh-
ing. The inlaws are naturally more reserved, waiting
until they get to *their* family's before flowering into rare
form. Mother and Dad sit at the head of the table and
beam.

Nana always has a huge box of presents to distribute—
with something for everyone. All of the children who are
taking piano lessons must perform. Carolyn must sing her
newest song, speak her newest piece, and tell her latest

joke. The little boys are coaxed into a rendition of "Jingle Bells," with Nana at the piano, urging them on. Without too much coaxing, my father will sing "Silent Night," followed up with his all-time favorite, "Open Up The Golden Gates To Dixie." Al will finally yield to Mother's urging and sing a song especially for her. My sister Rosemary will give us "O Holy Night" in a voice that seems to grow in beauty with each child. Finally, in one hoarse chorus of voices, we will sing through the songbook from beginning to end, while the little boys fight over which truck is whose, and the little girls stand near the treble keys of the piano sneaking in furtive little grace notes.

Around 7 P.M. we all try to be back home again. The house looks so cozy on Christmas evening with the outside lights glowing in the evergreens and the lovely tree in the corner of the living room casting a spell over all the familiar furniture. This is one of the few times of the year we feel leisurely enough to don robes and light the fire in the fireplace.

Inevitably, our coffee crew will begin appearing: Father Cahill (wearing a newer, louder sport shirt under his collar and bib), the Micaris or Murphys with some little gift from their house to ours, and sometimes, Father Malachy or Seamus. The children's friends are regular guests on Christmas night too; they wear their loot and help the children search for the Coke. Later on, over coffee and fruit cake, we may sing a little, or just sit before the fire and let the joy of the day drift into our consciousness to store up for another year.

E47